My Ducks Are Really Swans

My
DUCKS
Are Really
SWANS

Deanna Harrison

BROADMAN PRESS
Nashville, Tennessee

ISBN: 0-8054-5059-9
Dewey Decimal Classification: 248.4
Subject Heading: CHRISTIAN LIFE
Library of Congress Catalog Number: 88-6387
Printed in the United States of America

Unless otherwise stated, all Scripture quotations are from HOLY BIBLE: *New International Version,* copyright © 1978, New York Bible Society. Used by permission.
Scripture quotations marked RSV are from the Revised Standard Version of the Bible, copyrighted 1946, 1952, © 1971, 1973.
Scripture quotations marked Williams are from the *Williams New Testament, the New Testament in the Language of the People,* by Charles B. Williams. Copyright © 1937, 1966, 1986 by Holman Bible Publishers. Used by permission.

Library of Congress Cataloging-in-Publication Data

Harrison, Deanna, 1956-
   My ducks are really swans.

   1. Meditations.   I. Title.
BV4832.2.H3246   1988   242   88-6387
ISBN 0-8054-5059-9 (pbk.)

To my best friend and husband,
Scott.
Thank you for believing.

Contents

My Ducks Are Really Swans

My Ducks Are Really Swans

Close your eyes for a moment and let your imagination leisurely roam through the four seasons. Begin by feeling the sizzling hot days of summer followed by brisk autumn winds and crackling leaves. Now brace yourself for a brutally harsh winter of ice and snow—maybe a blizzard or two. But don't despair. A beautiful spring awaits just around the corner.

Spring: that glorious season when life is at its best. How would you describe a perfect spring day? What details would you include? A gentle breeze caressing fields of blossoming baby buds? Lying on a grassy hillside, bathed in the warmth of the sun's golden rays? Listening to the sweet melodies of a lark or watching a newborn calf take its first wobbly steps?

Perhaps your perfect spring day is set on the banks of a quiet, peaceful lake. Far off in the distance, sleek sailboats skim the horizon while several seasoned fishermen leave a hustle-and-bustle world behind as they enter a dimension understood only by them. High overhead a flock of birds fly effortlessly, breathing silent prayers of thanksgiving that they have survived hunting season once again. And far beneath them, sitting all alone in the placid water, is one sleepy duck dozing in the sunshine.

At least the feathered fowl appears to be a duck, but from this distance it's hard to tell. It might possibly be a swan. After all, they are members of the same bird family and have numerous physical features in common. For example, they both have flattened bills, webbed feet, and waterproof feathers. And both are good swimmers.

So what's the verdict? Is the bird in the middle of the lake a dozing duck or a snoozing swan? From this distance it's impossible to tell for certain. We'll have to get closer to see if it has a long, slender neck and long, pointed wings. We'll have to wake it up before we can hear whether it quacks like a duck or whistles the trumpetlike call of a swan. And it would be a tremendous help if we could see it take a few steps on land to determine its degree of gracefulness.

It's not always easy for an untrained eye to distinguish ducks from swans, chipmunks from squirrels, or harmless foliage from poison ivy. It often requires a second, third, or fourth glance, and sometimes a closer inspection.

And so it is in our day-to-day lives. At first glance a situation or event appears to be dull, boring, or to say the least, routine. Another is quickly chalked up as hopeless or useless while still others are labeled hardships, heartaches, or tragedies.

But take a second look, or maybe a third, or fourth. The situations we tend to overlook because of their familiarity are the very ones God uses to build our character. The events we consider to be hopeless are the ones He uses to strengthen our faith. And hardships, heartaches, and tragedies are the main ingredients He chooses to mold a spirit of endurance.

Life is not always what it seems. Sometimes, hidden within the ordinary lies an extraordinary truth simply waiting to be revealed. We must get closer, look longer, and listen more attentively. Only then will we discover that our ducks are really swans.

Room for Improvement

Alex Jefferson likes to make improvements. His garage is neatly organized with every conceivable tool necessary for plumbing, painting, construction, and electrical work. Alex always has at least one project in progress.

Most recently Alex's pet project was his daughter's bedroom. Not only did he paint the ceiling and walls, but he stripped, sanded, and revarnished the hardwood floor. Before beginning that project he had gutted and remodeled her bathroom: new tile, new fixtures, and new plumbing—the whole shebang. Alex loves to make improvements!

My father likes to make improvements. In his opinion, no automobile runs well enough to be left alone. There's always something that needs a little bit of tuning up. He's constantly changing spark plugs, cleaning air filters, tightening belts, draining oil, replacing oil, checking hoses, or rebuilding a carburetor. He even knocks out dents and puts on a fresh coat of paint whenever necessary. In fact, Dad's favorite pastime is buying old cars just so he can make repairs. He loves to make improvements!

Janet likes to make improvements. Her house is in a continual state of being changed and rearranged. The furniture is never in the same place two weeks in a row. Pictures are hung, rehung, and eventually make the full circle back to their original nails. The walls are always freshly painted, and the carpets never have the opportunity to show signs of dirt before they are steam cleaned—all in the name of improvement. Janet loves to make improvements.

My neighbor, Mr. Baker, loves to make improvements—much to the chagrin of those who live nearby. Mr. Baker's first love is his lawn. He never told me this in so many words, but his portion of the neighborhood makes it an obvious fact. Not a day goes by that he's not mowing, edging, trimming, planting, fertilizing, or spraying. His lawn is precisely manicured to perfection twelve months of the year. But Mr. Baker is never completely satisfied with how it appears. Whenever he isn't working in his yard, he's sitting on the front porch, surveying the situation, and deciding what should be done next. He loves to make improvements!

It's amazing how we become so enthusiastic about making external improvements. Americans spend millions of dollars each year on makeup, diet plans, exercise classes, designer clothing, false eyelashes, plastic fingernails, contemporary hairstyles, and a hodgepodge of fashion accessories. We'll invest almost any amount of money in virtually any product that promises to improve our outward condition.

But what about our internal condition? Is there room for spiritual improvement? The question is not whether you are a spiritual giant or a newborn babe. Regardless of where you are in your spiritual growth the question is the same: Is there room for improvement?

Undoubtedly the answer is yes. There will always be some new truth that God wants to teach us. There will always be ways in which we can become more like our Lord. *There's always room for spiritual improvement.*

So how can we go about making improvements on our spiritual lives? First, we must prayerfully evaluate where we stand with our Heavenly Father. How are our prayer lives and Bible study habits? Are we growing spiritually or are we beginning to stagnate? Take a moment now and jot down a few insights concerning your spiritual health.

_____

_____

_____

After you've determined your spiritual condition, consider the following ideas.

• Become involved in a weekly Bible study group. Actively participate in discussions and in-depth searching of the Scriptures.

• Establish a daily time of personal Bible study and prayer. Make it your own productive time with the Lord.

• Find a friend with whom you can study and pray. Encourage each other in your spiritual pilgrimages.

• Read books on prayer such as *Prayer: Life's Limitless Reach* by Jack Taylor and *The Power of Positive Praying* by John Bisagno.

• Take advantage of a variety of study courses offered through local churches, colleges, or seminaries.

• Read Christian books by a variety of authors from diverse backgrounds. Challenge your mind to consider new and different ideas as your spiritual life grows and matures.

• Investigate your church and public libraries. Make use of not only their books but their videocassettes as well.

• Develop a personal Bible study plan using commentaries and study course books. Check out your nearest Christian book store. Most of them carry a variety of inexpensive paperback study guides.

There's always room for spiritual improvement, regardless of age, education, or church background. Usually, it's when we think we don't need any improvement that we need it the most.

One evening, while attending a meeting promoting a witness-training seminar, I sat by a retired seminary professor. Throughout the meeting I kept wondering why Dr. Feather was there. He'd spent his entire life either ministering on church staffs or teaching others how to minister.

Perhaps Dr. Feather is going to speak or lead the closing prayer, I thought. He, of all people, certainly did not need to enroll in a course on how to witness. Yet when the time came to sign up, he was one of the first to commit himself to the seminar.

Why was Dr. Feather going to attend a course on witness training? Because he knew that we'll never learn all there is to be learned. We'll never be completely developed spiritually. Until Christ returns, and we are made perfect as He is perfect, lacking in nothing, there will always be room for improvement.

3

When Life Doesn't Make Sense

The church parking lot in Dallas, Texas, appeared to be the site of outright chaos. Usually covered with cars neatly filed in their designated slots, it was now buried under a sea of pillows, suitcases, garment bags, bedrolls, food, radios, and assorted stuffed animals.

One hundred or so people milled around and last-minute parental instructions could be heard throughout the crowd as every mother recited her list of DOs and DON'Ts one final time. All signs pointed to one thing. The church's youth choir was about to depart on yet another trip.

This particular trip, however, was different from all the others. The teenagers were not going to sing in schools, churches, or shopping malls. Nor were they going to conduct Vacation Bible Schools on the Rio Grande River. For the first time in history, the Texas prison system had agreed to allow the teenagers to sing for the inmates.

The choir had practiced and prayed for months in preparation for their trip. Finally, the day arrived and their excitement knew no bounds. It was a dream come true.

At last the bus was loaded and everyone paused for a moment of prayer. Then the parents and friends stepped back and waved good-bye as the bus slowly chugged its way out of the parking lot. "Be careful . . . . We love you . . . . Call us when you get there . . . . Obey your sponsors . . . . Take care of your sister."

The bus drove out of sight and the parents headed home, content to know that their children were destined for prison. The vacant parking lot was quiet once again, but not for long.

Less than six hours had passed, but the teenagers' parents found themselves gathered once more. This time, however, there was no laughter—only muffled cries mixed with intense, unspeakable sorrow and stunned disbelief. The bus pulled slowly onto the parking lot and the teenagers quietly, numbly stepped off—all except one.

The small town of Granbury had been the site of the group's first stop. The bus needed refueling and by that time the hungry youth were ready to raid the vending machines. The small gas station, however, wasn't prepared for such a large group, especially one with such ravenous appetites, so some of the teenagers headed across the highway to a nearby grocery store. Nothing unusual. It was done on every trip.

But this time tragedy struck. For some unexplainable reason Becky didn't see the oncoming truck until it was too late. The screeching tires and screams of horror were futile. Death was immediate.

The question we all asked was: "Why?" Why had God allowed such a tragedy to happen? This was not a bunch of wild kids on some sort of destructive spree. These were not disrespectful malcontents. These were good kids, Christian kids, on their way to share the gospel of Jesus Christ. They had given their time and money in order to share His message, to do His work. They were carrying out their part to fulfill a God-given dream.

But their dream had turned into a nightmare. Why had God not intervened? Surely He could have prevented Becky's death by any means He chose. So why hadn't He?

In all honesty, God never answered. He brought good from the tragedy, and He gave strength to endure the pain. But He never explained why He had not prevented the accident.

There are many times in life when difficult circumstances and unbearable heartaches occur. Illness, financial impossibilities, divorce, loss of a job, betrayal by friends, death of a loved one—life simply doesn't make sense. And more often than not, God doesn't provide a satisfactory explanation.

Though God does not always answer our whys, and though life often doesn't make sense, the Scriptures do offer an explanation to God's lack of explanations. It's found in Isaiah 55:8-11:

> For my thoughts are not your thoughts,
> neither are your ways my ways, ...
> As the heavens are higher than the earth,
> so are my ways higher than your ways
> and my thoughts than your thoughts (vv. 8-9).

In addition to an explanation of God's silence, the Scriptures also offer an abundance of strength, comfort, and hope. Consider again the words of the prophet Isaiah:

> So do not fear, for I am with you;
> do not be dismayed, for I am your God.
> I will strengthen you and help you;
> I will uphold you with my righteous right hand (41:10).

The psalmist said, "The Lord is a refuge for the oppressed,/a stronghold in times of trouble./for you, Lord, have never forsaken those who seek you" (9:9-10). Again he said, "O Lord my God, I called to you for help/and you healed me . . . weeping may remain for a night,/but rejoicing comes in the morning" (30:2,5).

And it is our own Lord who urges us: "Come to me, all you who are weary and burdened, and I will give you rest" (Matt.

11:28). Later He said, "Do not let your hearts be troubled. Trust in God; trust also in me" (John 14:1).

While God's Word may not always provide the answers we want or think we deserve, it never fails to offer strength and comfort. When life makes no sense at all, when the pain seems too intense to bear, God steps in and takes over.

It was in the strength of Almighty God that the youth choir was able to triumphantly sing at Becky's funeral. It had just been three days since their friend had died, and their grief was undeniable. But the words that they sang gave them strength to accept life, even though it made no sense. Through tears and sadness their voices proclaimed: "God is so wonderful. I can't explain. But I can say, 'Glory, hallelujah! Praise His holy name.' "

4

You Don't Say

Small towns confuse me. You'd think you'd be able to find your way around in them, but not so. At least I can't. Put me in downtown Dallas with a city map and I can get just about anywhere. But put me in a small town with home folks' directions on how to get somewhere, and I'll be lost in sixty seconds flat.

Believe me, I know what I'm talking about. We lived in a small town for over four years, and I never did get the hang of things. Up until the day we moved there I had been accustomed to following directions such as: "Drive four blocks north and turn right on Third Street. Follow Third Street for two and one-half miles and turn left. The address is 4313."

Directions of that kind do not exist in a small town. Instead it's "Go out past the Bakers' old home place. (The Bakers haven't lived there for thirty years and I, being new to town, have no idea who the Bakers are to begin with.) A little ways after you pass their house, turn left on the dirt road when the main road curves. Then turn again at the oak tree and follow the gravel road until you come to a stock tank—the big one, not the little one. Turn right about a half mile past the stock tank. You can't miss it."

Wanna bet?

Recently, while visiting a fairly small town I needed a particular brand of paint. After several stops I discovered that only one store in town carried that brand. The instructions I received on how to find that store went something like this:

"To get to Weakley-Watson's you need to go to the traffic circle and bear to the right. Then turn left on Fisk Street. After, oh, one or two traffic lights you'll come to the old Weakley-Watson's store. Turn there, and you'll see their new store behind it."

With those instructions I set out to find Weakley-Watson's Store. After touring the traffic circle, I eventually located Fisk Street and began looking for the old store. Up one side and down the other, I cruised Fisk Street for a good six or seven minutes while reading every sign, every marquee. But none bore the name Weakley-Watson.

Finally, out of boredom and desperation, I turned down a side street, and there it was. The new Weakley-Watson's. It was a True Value Hardware Store! Why, I'd passed the old True Value store half a dozen times on Fisk Street, but no one had bothered to tell me that Weakley-Watson's was a True Value Hardware Store! Apparently that was a minor fact to the hometown people, but to a foreigner it was a mighty important detail.

Have you ever noticed how often we fail to include what seem to be minor details? Details like: *I love you. You're special. You sure look nice today. I appreciate you. You did a great job. Please. Thank you. I'm sorry.*

We forget that other people can't read our thoughts. They can't see the mental maps that clearly show the way from our hearts to our minds. If we think it or feel it, we need to say it.

Years ago there was a television game show called "You Don't Say." The object of the game was for one player to give a clue sentence in order to prompt one's partner to say a specific phrase. The trick was to say as much as possible in the clue without saying the key thought.

Sometimes it seems as though we're habitually playing "You

Don't Say." We give many clues but never really state what we want the other person to know. Couples who are dating do this frequently. Each wonders what the other is feeling, but they aren't brave enough to put their feelings into words. So they continue playing "You Don't Say," wondering if they're winning or losing the game.

Several years ago I read about a man named Phil who had just learned that his best friend had died. The two men had been friends for many years—ever since their school days. Though they had moved far apart geographically they had occasionally kept in touch, mostly through Christmas cards.

But the Christmas cards provided little consolation when Phil learned of his friend's death. Instead, a letter haunted his time of grief. The letter talked about how special the men's friendship had been down through the years. It mentioned memorable moments that the friends had experienced. One sentence clearly stated that the friendship meant more than words could adequately express.

It was a beautiful letter. Every line was packed with meaning. Why did it haunt Phil? Because he had written it to his friend but had never found the time to mail it. Phil had waited too long to say what he really felt.

Had King Solomon known Phil, he would have insisted that the letter be mailed before time ran out. Solomon knew the importance of words. In Proverbs he wrote, "Pleasant words are a honeycomb,/sweet to the soul and healing to the bones" (16:24).

Pleasant, sweet, healing words—they're too important to leave unspoken. Nor do they deserve to be left at the mercy of game-show tactics. Forget about giving clever clues. The other person may not even know the rules of the game. If you feel it or think it, then say it. That's the only rule you need to remember.

5

Meeting of the Minds

When I was a senior in high school my best friend and I had the thrill of hearing the famous piano duo Ferrante and Teicher in concert. In their own unique style they mesmerized the audience as they made the two grand pianos come to life. For more than two hours we sat spellbound, watching the duo perform as one.

It's no wonder the men think and play as one. They've been playing the piano together since they were six years old when, while students at the Juilliard School of Music in New York City, they chose each other as partners. For more than fifty years Arthur Ferrante and Louis Teicher have worked together, studied together, practiced together, traveled together, and performed together. They know each other's minds.

Knowing someone else's mind is not unique to the world of musicians. It also plays a key role in the realm of athletics. From 1947 until 1964, Bud Wilkinson was the head football coach at the University of Oklahoma. During that time the Sooners were known for a consistent winning record and won numerous national championships. Interestingly enough, Wilkinson did not call the plays from the sideline. He was known throughout college football as the coach who allowed his quarterback to call the plays on the field.

When asked how he could get away with allowing his quarterback to call the plays, Wilkinson explained his strategy. Throughout the year, on the field and off, the coach lived with his quarterback. He implanted his philosophy of football into the student's mind as he taught him everything he knew and believed about the game. They spent countless hours together studying football strategies and plays.

One teaching aid Coach Wilkinson used was a little blackboard that he carried with him at all times. Frequently, he created a situation on the board and instructed the quarterback to explain what he thought should be done. After the young student finished, the experienced coach would say, "Now here's what I would do."

By the time football season rolled around, the quarterback no longer thought like a quarterback. He viewed each game like a coach. The plays he called on the field were not the plays of a quarterback's mind. Instead, he selected each play as Coach Wilkinson had trained him to do.

But, as fate would have it, Coach Wilkinson eventually came face-to-face with his match. Darrell Royal, football coach at the University of Texas, beat Wilkinson on three different occasions. He was the only coach who could ever make that claim.

Why were Darrell Royal's Texas Longhorns able to beat Bud Wilkinson's Oklahoma Sooners? Simple. When the two teams met on the field, Coach Royal did not call the plays as Darrell Royal. He called them as Bud Wilkinson. You see, Darrell Royal had once played for Bud Wilkinson as quarterback. Years later, in every situation, he knew how his opponent would think and respond. He knew the older man's mind.[1]

Knowing someone's mind doesn't come easily or by accident. Consider the couple who has been married for over fifty years. They've spent so much time together and have experienced so many joys and sorrows that they've become more and more like each other. They think alike, talk alike, and even walk alike.

They have the same goals, desires, and interests. Most of the time they know what each other is thinking without asking. They know each other's mind.

All of these people have one thing in common. They know someone else extremely well as a result of spending many long hours together.

Many times I sit in amazement as I watch my husband Scott interact with the teenagers of our community. Often I get the feeling that they are speaking in a foreign language when I fail to recognize the names and places they refer to in conversation.

But Scott understands teenagers. His love for youth motivates him to listen and learn to communicate. He knows the authors they read, the music they listen to, and the movies they see. He knows their interests, their temptations, and their desires as a result of spending time with them. They eat together, play together, study together, talk together, and travel together. It's no wonder Scott knows their minds.

My relationship to God is based upon that same principle. If I am to have a close personal relationship with Him then I must spend time with Him. Lots of time. Time in His Word. Time in prayer. Time in meditation. Time with His people.

Knowing more about the mind of God only comes with time. The more time I spend with Him, the more I understand His desires and will for my life. The more time I spend talking with Him, the more I understand what He's trying to teach me. If I am ever to know His thoughts I must spend many hours in His presence. Only then will I gain a glimpse of His mind.

Note

1. Coaching illustration taken from cassette tape entitled "Leadership and Motivation" by Herschel Creasman, Tape 10, Side B, produced by the cassette ministry of First Baptist Church, Dallas.

6

Details, Details

It's amazing how one relatively small piece of jewelry can totally change a female's personality. A basically sane individual goes through changes that even Jekyll and Hyde never experienced. And all because some starry-eyed guy gave her a ring and popped the big question.

Brides-to-be: they're a unique species all their own. For literally years they've been dreaming of their weddings, and now that they've answered yes to the big question they begin months of preparation for the all-important event.

If you've never had the pleasure of being in on preparing for a wedding, or perhaps it's been so long ago that you've forgotten what it was actually like, let me refresh your memory.

First of all, there are seven basic areas of preparation: the engagement, bridal showers, rehearsal, wedding ceremony, wedding reception, honeymoon, and the happily-ever-after phase.

Decisions must be made concerning announcements, proper attire, thank-you notes, guests lists, photographers, rings, food, attendants, attendants' clothing, flowers, order of ceremony, invitations, honeymoon, reception, and setting up the new home. And that barely skims the surface.

Details, details, details! How did a simple thing like getting married ever become so complicated? It's no wonder that the bride-to-be and her mother spend months running hither and yon, talking of nothing else but the wedding, spending money with no thought of tomorrow. (It's Dad's job to think of tomorrow!) Suddenly eloping doesn't sound like such a bad idea after all.

That's enough about weddings. Have you ever been closely associated with someone who is expecting a baby? I don't mean have you just *known* someone who is expecting. Have you ever gone through the nine-month ordeal from start to finish? The number of details is astronomical! The financial deposits and requirements from the obstetrician, lab technicians, radiologists, pediatrician, and hospital are mind boggling.

And then there are the positive, enjoyable details: decorating the nursery, choosing a name, and sending out birth announcements. Often it seems that nine months is nowhere near enough time to prepare for a baby.

Weddings, births, graduations. There are many occasions that occur throughout life that are loaded with thousands of tiny little details. But the occasions are not always joyous. Sometimes they're scary, nerveracking, and the cause of many a sleepless night: funerals, job hunting, and the ordeal of moving.

In the fall of 1983 my husband and I experienced one of those nerve-racking events: moving. We spent one weekend with a realtor looking at numerous houses for sale in San Angelo, Texas. At the end of the third day after signing a contract on a house, we returned to Dallas where we began the packing process.

There was only one minor detail that caused a bit of stress. We still owned our house in Dallas. The bottom line was—*we owned two houses!* While owning a house was one of my life's dreams, owning two houses was a nightmare!

Eventually, everything worked out. We sold the house, made

the move, and lived to tell about it. There were times, however, when the details seemed insurmountable to us. But not to God. He specializes in details.

Take the birth of Christ, for example. Now there was an event chock-full of details. Imagine orchestrating Mary and Joseph's engagement and wedding, the trip to Bethlehem, the angels' announcement, or the visits of the shepherds and Wise Men. The escape to Egypt. Talk about details!

But now consider the birth of Christ from Mary's perspective. Mary only knew a few of the details. She knew nothing about the specifics of her child's birth. She knew nothing about the overcrowded inns and cattle stall, the angelic announcement, the shepherds on the hillside, or God's miraculous intervention through the Wise Men to halt Herod's plan. Mary only saw God's details as He revealed them to her.

We, too, can only see God's details as He chooses to reveal them to us. And often He chooses to reveal very little. We rarely know what's going to happen next. The whats, whys, hows, and wherefores are not spelled out in clear, precise terms.

But regardless of what we don't know, we can still find hope in the knowledge that we serve a God whose wisdom and power far exceed human comprehension. Even though we are unable to see the outcome, we can put all of the details of our lives in the hands of our almighty God. Only He can make sense of them. Only He can perfectly orchestrate the events that touch our lives. And He is able to do it all with very little difficulty, for we serve a God who specializes in details.

7

Why?

Anyone who has children, grandchildren, or has ever worked with little ones knows that there are specific stages of childhood development. While each one is special and exciting, some stages require more patience and understanding than others. One such stage is the *why* stage.

The *why* stage begins innocently enough one day with a simple question—*Why?* The method of questioning soon develops into "Why not?" and "How come?" but the message remains basically the same.

In the beginning, *why* questions are asked out of genuine curiosity. At some point in time, however, I sincerely believe children often ask *why* out of a sadistic desire to see a parent, teacher, or some other pitiful adult struggle to come up with a satisfactory answer.

Many times a child will first ask an innocent question—one that might possibly have an answer. But watch out! Your perfectly phrased answer is sure to be met with another *why?* For example, after creatively answering questions such as: "Does Jesus wash His hair?" or "Do dead bugs go to heaven?" the next question will automatically be: *Why?* or *Why not?* All in all, it's quite a learning experience for adult and child alike.

From my own experience in working with children I've come to three conclusions about *why* questions. The first is that sometimes a child will ask *why* but not really be interested in the answer. This is based upon the number of times the child becomes distracted by something else before I've had a chance to reply.

The second conclusion concerning *why* questions is that when children don't like an answer they receive, they keep asking *why* in the hope that the answer will eventually change. This often leads to exasperation for everyone. I mean, there are just so many ways you can answer: "Why can't I have my chocolate cake before supper?" But the persistent child will most certainly keep asking.

The third conclusion is, for me, the most frustrating. The frustration stems from the fact that there are times when a child simply cannot comprehend the answer to his question, regardless of how well the answer is worded. Someday, after the child grows and develops further, he might be able to clearly understand the answer. But though the adult knows that, the child still asks *why* in an effort to grasp the unknown.

I vividly recall one day in particular when my two-year-old voiced two years' worth of pent-up questions. She asked everything from "Why can't you put the peeling back on the apple?" to "What do people do in heaven?" Each answer, of course, was followed by an endless barrage of *whys*.

Though my child's questions far exceeded my wisdom, I was determined to answer each one to her satisfaction. By the end of the day my brain was exhausted, and my ears throbbed as *why* reverberated throughout my head. Never in my wildest dreams had I imagined one little girl could ask so many questions in just one day's time.

It wasn't until late that night, as I briefed my husband on the day's events, that the Lord opened my eyes to see myself. Suddenly I heard echoes of my own voice repeatedly hounding

God with endless questions. And, in all honesty, I have to admit that many of my questions are just like those of a child.

Some of my questions, for example, don't need answers. Nor do I hang around to hear the answer should one be given. In haste I express my thoughts and opinions to the Lord, ask a few questions, then rush on to the next activity of the day. It's amazing how often I don't wait to hear God's reply.

At other times my questions receive answers that I just don't like. Why, for example, was one area of my life not progressing as it should? The answer: pride. Again I asked why and again the answer came back: pride. *But there must be another reason,* I thought. I refused to admit that I harbored pride in my life. So once again I asked why. And again. And again, until finally I accepted God's answer and painfully acknowledged the presence of pride.

And finally, like the questions of a child, the most frustrating questions that I ask God are those whose answers are beyond my comprehension. Why, for example, did God allow a little boy to suffer from a bizarre case of meningitis and ultimately lose his arms and legs as a result of severe complications?

Why did God allow another little boy to have a brain tumor and undergo surgery and painful chemotherapy?

Why does He allow extreme proverty, starvation, and mental retardation?

And why did God allow John Faught to die?

John Faught was a rare man—the kind you only meet once in a lifetime, if that often. He was the kind of man who made his corner of the world a better place just by being there. John was a man of compassion and integrity. His life's purpose and goal was to serve his God while loving other people. And daily he met that goal.

Our society needs a lot more people like John Faught: people who will live love when surrounded by hate, people who will speak honestly while surrounded by lies and deceit. There seems to be a shortage of such persons. Surely God could use a thousand more.

But God chose a different path. So when word came that John Faught had suddenly died, the question we all asked was: WHY? Why did God take such a saint from our presence? Why did He leave a beautiful wife and two wonderful children without their husband and father? Why?

I must admit that God never answered any of those questions, though I've asked Him repeatedly. I want to understand; I'm just not able. My finite mind is not capable of comprehending the infinite reasoning of Almighty God.

And, finally, there are times when I ask God *why* that He simply answers, "Wait, My child. You cannot understand My ways at this time in your life." And then, after a period of waiting and maturing, God reveals His answer: but never before I am able to comprehend it.

One such period of waiting occurred years ago when I was in college. When I was the tender age of nineteen the young man I had planned to marry abruptly ended our relationship. I was devastated. My dreams were shattered, and my aching prayer was one brief word: *Why?*

While God healed the wounds and put the pieces of my life back in place, He didn't explain why He'd allowed me to experience such pain. For nearly two years He was silent when I asked *why.* And then one day I was finally ready for His answer. It came on June 3 when I was introduced to the young ministerial student I would eventually marry.

There are times when I suspect that my child lays awake at night dreaming up questions to ask the following day. Though her days of questioning are often exhausting, I hope this phase of her life never completely ends. I hope her curiosity will always motivate her to learn and grow.

In the same way, God wants us to bring our questions to Him. We are commanded to ask, to seek, and to knock. We are urged to make our requests known, and that includes requests for wisdom, understanding, and insight. Often these things are the product of a brief, one-word prayer: *Why?*

8

Sailing on the Seas of Life

In my husband's office there hangs a beautiful picture of a small ship docked in a harbor at sunset. The water is smooth and tranquil, free from turbulent waves or gusty winds. The scene is serenity at its best. The caption across the bottom, however, reads, "A ship in the harbor is safe. But that is not what ships are built for."

Without exception, every ship is built with a purpose in mind. There are commercial ships to transport cargo, luxury liners for entertainment and sheer pleasure, as well as boats designed for racing and fishing.

And then there are boats for everyday folks: boats with sails or outboard motors. But even among sailboats there is a vast variety from which to choose. How about a dinghy, a schooner, or a ketch? A yawl or a catboat? Some sailboats are made for Saturday sailing, some for family cruising, and still others are powerful enough to be used in competition.

You say you don't want to depend upon the wind for your boating pleasure? Then outboard motors may be the solution. There are speedsters for racing and runabouts for water skiing and fishing. And don't forget the small family cruisers, utility boats, and—for the person who really wants to get away from it all—the houseboat.

From the smallest dinghy to the military warship, each has

a responsibility, a standard of performance to meet or exceed. And though many vessels appear to be vastly different, they all have one thing in common—each one was created for a purpose. Not one was built to spend its life snuggly secured in the harbor.

A ship in the harbor is safe. But that is not what ships are built for.

I've never been able to look at the picture in my husband's office without feeling uneasy. Its penetrating message always convicts me of my desire to lead a tranquil, hassle-free life. But is that what I was created for? Is it really possible to serve the Lord without sailing the stormy seas of life as He did?

In reality, the seas of the Christian life are often plagued by the high winds of persecution and the jagged rocks of suffering. Let's face it. It's tough to stand up for Christian convictions and principles when society urges us to live by its own perverted standards. Why not settle for the "good life" here on earth? You only live once, you know. And if you live your one life according to Christ's example, things are going to get a little rough.

The disciples discovered the rough seas of following Christ one evening in the middle of a lake. After a long exhausting day of teaching, Christ suggested that they travel to the other side of the lake. Grateful for an excuse to escape the multitudes, the disciples piled into their boat and set sail across the Sea of Galilee.

But the small band of men soon had a change of heart when a fierce storm suddenly whipped up the lake. The whirling, twisting winds created such turbulent waves that they beat against the boat and tossed it violently across the sea. Fear became unadulterated panic when water began filling the small vessel. The terrified disciples thought surely they were doomed.

Finally, in the midst of the storm, they turned to Christ who was sleeping in the stern. Upon being awakened by His near-hysterical men, Christ spoke to the raging winds and waves. Immediately the sea was calm (see Mark 4:35-41).

We, like the disciples, often become terrified by the storms of life. The roaring winds and torrential rains of fear, temptation, insecurity, heartache, worry, illness, rejection, and loneliness seem to overwhelm our small vessels. As the winds increase and the dark clouds roll in, we're tempted to hightail it back to shore. Let somebody else maneuver the storm. Let someone else sail through the treacherous waters. We're going back to the shelter on the shore.

But notice where Christ was during the storm. He was in the boat *with* His disciples. He wasn't on the shore, safe and sound. He didn't yell words of encouragement from dry ground.

Christ doesn't call the plays of our lives from the sidelines. He doesn't tell us how to land the plane via radio while sitting secure in a control tower. He doesn't explain how to transverse the mountainous terrain while sipping hot chocolate beside the fireplace in a ski lodge. He doesn't teach us how to swim while perched on a lifeguard's roost.

No. Christ lives our lives *with* us. He was right smack dab in the middle of the rolling waves of the Sea of Galilee that night long ago, and He is right in the middle of the storms of our lives today. Whatever the weather conditions, Christ is there. Whether it's a spring shower or a vicious tornado, He is sailing through the storm beside us giving strength and guidance, helping adjust our sails, ensuring that we make it through to the other side.

A ship in the harbor may be safe, but that is not what a ship is built for. While we may occasionally attempt to hide from the storms of life, God never intended for us to live in cushy comfort. He created us for much more than that.

God created us to serve Him, to follow His will, and to daily become more like His Son. We can hardly fulfill that purpose if we are safely, snuggly anchored on shore. Instead we must set our sails, adjust our course, and acknowledge Christ as Captain of our vessels. Then we must keep right on sailing through the seas of life, even if the forecast calls for rain.

9

Fuel for Faith

Someone perfectly summed up my car in one brief phrase. It's on a bumper sticker that says, "From 0-60 in 15 minutes."

That describes my car in a nutshell: four doors, four wheels, and four cylinders. My husband calls it the Wimpmobile. A consumer guidebook on used cars describes the motor as "feeble." Other terms like lethargic, decrepit, and comatose also pop to mind.

Nevertheless, my little car takes care of my needs about 90 percent of the time, and that's not too bad I suppose. Luckily I live in a city whose goal is to preserve a small-town atmosphere by keeping the speed limits at 40 miles per hour or less. As long as I stay on my well-beaten paths in town I'm safe. But a trip of any extended distance is another story.

I first experienced the major drawback of my little car on a trip to San Antonio. The 215 miles can best be described by one simple word: hilly. It didn't take long to discover that I had to hit the bottom of a hill going at least 65 miles per hour if I had any desire to ever see the top. With my foot pressed to the floor the speedometer steadily dropped from 65 to 40 before we reached level ground.

The Wimpmobile may be sufficient for the routine demands of everyday life, but when the road gets steep, forget it. The slightest incline will catch it off guard. It just doesn't have what it takes.

It struck me one day that my faith is often like my car. It's sufficient for a day's usual demands, and it's strong enough to get me through the small ordeals of life. But should a mountain arise, I may quickly run out of gas.

There is one good thing about my car. It gets terrific gas mileage. It requires very little fuel to keep it going while my husband's eight-cylinder car burns a great deal more.

Another way of looking at the comparison, however, is that my little car, with its little bit of fuel, has very little power. My husband's big car, on the other hand, with its big fuel consumption, has enough power to leave me choking in his dust.

So it is with faith. A prayer here and there and an occasional Bible study may keep our faith strong enough for daily routines. But a faith capable of climbing the mountains that suddenly arise requires a lot more fuel than that.

Fuel for faith: that's what we need. The strength and power to face difficult situations lies in the fuels of God's Word and communion with Him through prayer. And forget about good gas mileage. Drink in all the fuel you can. You never know what mountains you'll have to climb.

10

Failure Need Not Be Fatal

If any of the following men were contestants on the television game show: "Symbol of Success," it's highly unlikely that any of them would win even a consolation prize. Just listen to parts of their biographical sketches:

Contestant Number One has more power than he knows what to do with. Because of his powerful and prestigious position he has acquaintances in all walks of life who will do whatever he wishes. Recently, though, Contestant Number One had an affair with one such acquaintance. He's in a mighty fine fix now. Not only is the woman married, but her husband is one of his employees.

Contestant Number Two is frequently seen about town with royalty, but he has not yet learned to control his anger, at least not all of the time. Not long ago he killed a man. For a brief period of time he thought that he was the only one who knew about the murder. There were witnesses, however, and Contestant Number Two is now wanted by the law and has fled to another country.

Contestant Number Three recently gave in to discouragement and had a critical bout with depression. At one moment he was on top of the world with everything under control. Then, as the result of a couple of setbacks, he sank into the pits of depression. In fact he was so depressed that he hoped he would die! Wouldn't you like to have him at your next party?

Contestant Number Four is a deceiver and a thief. He uses whatever means necessary to get exactly what he wants. He's been known to catch people when they're down and use their weaknesses for his own gain. He didn't even mind taking advantage of his blind, elderly father. Currently, Contestant Number Four has fled the country due to threats on his life.

Contestant Number Five does not take orders well. He would not make an ideal recruit for the marine corps. Recently, he deliberately disobeyed a direct order from his commander. Due to bad weather and a breakdown in communications we have not been able to reach him for further comment.

Contestant Number Six constantly makes errors in judgment. These are basically caused by a severe case of immaturity which has alienated him from his peers. Don't you know he's fun to be around?

Contestant Number Seven is a nice enough guy if he's on your side. But if the two of you disagree, you'd better watch out. He is currently fighting those who oppose him and his views by killing them in an effort to exterminate what he considers to be the enemy.

Now which one of these guys would get your vote as the symbol of success? The adulterer or murderer? The guy who's so depressed that he wants to die? The deceitful thief? The renegade malcontent? How about the immature pest or the annihilator?

None of these men are what we would consider to be success stories. At least not based on what we've just heard about them. Yet David, Moses, Elijah, Jacob, Jonah, Joseph, and Paul all overcame their moments of failure and were used by God in mighty ways.

The key factor in these men's lives is that they did not allow their failures to be fatal. Too often we make the mistake of seeing ourselves rather than our actions as failures. Actions can fail; situations may be total flops; decisions may be 100-percent wrong; or events may be classified as complete washouts. *But people are never failures.*

Failure, painful though it may be, is an inevitable part of life. Many years ago Theodor Geisel, better known as Dr. Seuss, wrote a children's book entitled: *And to Think That I Saw It On Mulberry Street.* It was rejected by twenty-three publishers before he received a favorable reply and a contract from Vanguard Press. The book has since had over twenty printings.

Another author, Richard Bach, came face to face with failure eighteen times as eighteen publishers refused to accept *Jonathan Livingston Seagull.* Finally, in 1970, Macmillan published the book. Only five years later it had sold more than seven million copies in the United States alone.

And have you ever heard of the play *Green Grow the Lilacs?* Maybe not. It was considered a complete failure. But it was the basis for the Rodgers and Hammerstein musical *Oklahoma!*

Since failure is unavoidable we might as well make use of it. Anyone who properly handles successes has learned to properly face moments of failure. Each time we experience failure in our lives there are at least three lessons we can learn.

First, failure shows us our weak spots. In flashing neon lights it points out for us, and sometimes for the whole world, exactly what we need to work on and where improvements can be made.

Secondly, failure gives us a point from which to measure our improvements. We can look back over past failures and see that, though we may not have yet reached our goal, we've come a long way. And in the process we've enjoyed numerous mini-successes here and there.

Finally, failure reminds us that we must rely upon the power of God if we are to succeed in life. In our own feeble strength we can do nothing. Without God's help we inevitably fall flat on our faces. But with God's power we can do anything.

Christ promised that His power is perfected in weakness (see 2 Cor. 12:9). It's when we admit our feebleness and failures that our Lord empowers us with His might. That's why the great apostle Paul was never ashamed to acknowledge his own human limitations. In fact, he found strength in admitting his weaknesses.

"For when I am weak," Paul declared, "then I am strong" (2 Cor. 12:10b).

11

Easy Etiquette

Not long ago my husband and I had dinner at one of our favorite Italian restaurants. Luigi's is a small one-room building crammed wall to wall with red-checkered covered tables, rickety wooden chairs, and jolly waitresses who've obviously enjoyed too much of their own pasta. While waiting for their orders, diners can watch the chefs prepare their food in the kitchen or listen to a variety of conversations at surrounding tables.

On this particular evening Scott and I were seated so close to the couple at the next table that we appeared to be a party of four. A packet of sugar substitute could not have slipped between the two tables. I remember this dinner, not because of the tasty food but because of the tasteless conversation at the adjoining table.

When we arrived at our seats, the man at the next table was deeply engrossed in describing a recent experience. His date looked rather pale, and I soon discovered why. The man had recently undergone surgery and was now giving his poor companion a play-by-play review, sound effects and all. She never said a word throughout the entire dinner. She didn't eat much either.

Etiquette was not one of this man's strong points. He blatantly disobeyed page 233 of *Amy Vanderbilt's New Complete Book of Etiquette.* At the time, I hadn't read page 233, but instinct told me his dinner topic was all wrong.

Amy Vanderbilt has a lot to say about etiquette. In fact, it takes her 706 pages to instruct folks like me in how to meet, greet, and eat.

Now, I've never been a slob. I mean, I can hold my own at formal dinners. That's easy enough to do. I just spot a woman with obvious social graces and mimic her every move. But I'd never stopped to consider some of Amy's rules. For example:

• handshakes should be brief, firm, and at elbow level; (I don't know what you're supposed to do if there's a distinctive difference in height. It could pose a serious problem.)

• you should look the person squarely in the eye when you're shaking hands;

• a man should never extend his hand to a woman unless she has first extended hers;

• a man should not greet a woman until she has first given a sign of recognition;

• a man should not offer his arm to a woman during the daytime, only at night or in case of bad weather.

Eating out according to Amy's guidelines is a whole new experience. Consider these points:

• When there is only one wall seat, the woman sits there and the man takes the aisle seat.

• When two couples eat together, the women take the wall seats and the men sit in the aisle seats.

• When a younger couple eats with an older couple, the older couple should have the wall seats and the younger couple the aisle seats. Of course, the younger man should seat himself opposite the older woman. But you probably already knew that.

Now, if you don't feel like a social slob by this time, just read on. Your turn is coming. See if you incorporate all of these nifty rules into your daily eating habits:

• A soup or dessert dish may be tipped only if it is tipped away from the spoon and not toward the eater.

• Gravy should be put on meat only. (It's considered an insult to the cuisine to pour gravy over the vegies.)

• The salt and pepper should always be passed together. They should never be separated. (Hot dog! I knew that rule a long time ago!)

• When holding a cup with a handle, the pinky finger should curve in the same direction as the other fingers. It should not stand out snootily.

• Very crisp bacon may be eaten with your fingers, but otherwise you must use a fork and knife.

• When eating corn on the cob, butter and season only a row or two at a time—never the whole ear at once. How in the world you're supposed to eat one row of corn off the cob at a time is beyond me. You're going to look pretty silly, that's for sure. My rule of etiquette on this point is to only eat corn on the cob at home when no one else is around and the dental floss is handy.

See what I mean? How does anyone remember so many rules, regulations, and subsequent variations? And I haven't even read the chapters entitled "Employer-Servant Relations," "Dress and Duties of the Household Staff," "Your Press Relations," "Visiting West Point," and "An Audience with the Pope."

Most folks don't need to know all 706 pages of Amy Vanderbilt's guide to the social graces. Of course, we need help here and there, and we'd be foolish to ignore the basic standards of etiquette. But what about simple daily living?

Many of us aren't concerned with employer-servant relations, but we are involved in family relations and various job relations. We may never have an audience with the Pope or meet the president of the United States, but our lives do cross the paths of neighbors, mail carriers, store clerks, and gas station attendants. What rules do we have to guide us through our daily routines?

Christ knew we'd need help. And He also knew we wouldn't be able to remember a bunch of lengthy rules. Nor would we always be able to refer to a handy reference guide. So He made etiquette easy. In one brief sentence He summed up the whole ball of wax: "Do to others as you would have them do to you" (Luke 6:31).

Now that's etiquette made easy. The tough part is putting it into practice.

12

Perspective on Pain

"Wouldn't it be wonderful if we never felt pain? Just imagine. You could cut your finger without it hurting. You could exercise all you needed or wanted without every muscle in your body aching. You could have someone be hateful to you without feeling their hate."

Such was one young woman's perspective on pain. At first glance it looks like a good idea. How wonderful it would be to only have happy, positive experiences. Or would the absence of pain really be all that wonderful? Let's take a closer look at the idea of a pain-free life. What would life without pain really be like?

Life without pain would be life without courage, faith, or hope. These qualities are not products of a pampered carefree life but rather a life filled with downs as well as ups, bad as well as good, pain as well as progress.

Several years ago my husband and I were called to the hospital room of a dear friend who was facing cancer surgery. Myrtle was truly a godly woman. For three years I had loved and deeply respected her. She had an amazing faith and courageous spirit like few people possess. As we tried to offer comfort it was she who comforted and strengthened us.

Myrtle's strength was not something she had inherited. It was the product of pain—the pain of losing two husbands and a ten-year-old daughter in death. Through a series of events that could have resulted in hopeless despair, Myrtle discovered a deeper, more meaningful courage, faith, and hope as the pain of her life drove her closer to her Lord. Thank God for pain.

Life without pain would be life full of danger. Imagine having a broken leg, an inflamed appendix, or a heart attack without knowing it. That's an absurd thought, but it's exactly what would happen if our lives were free of pain. We would never know when our lives were in danger. We would have no warning of impending peril. We would be defenseless.

While physical pain warns us when our health is in danger, emotional pain warns us when relationships need extra care and attention. It's pain that signals the need for an apology and forgiveness. It's pain that signals the need to say, "Let's talk about this."

Around our house, summer is the most hectic season of the year. The rat race is endless, and the rats usually have the lead. My minister-husband and I spend less and less time at home and more and more time on the road, though we don't always travel the same roads.

Last summer, by mid July, when we no longer recognized each other as we passed in the kitchen, it was a deep, stabbing pain that caused us to say, "Hey, wait a minute! Something needs to change." It was that pain that motivated us to alter and rearrange our schedules in order to spend a few more hours together. Thank God for pain.

Life without pain would be life without growth. Perhaps two of the greatest examples of growing through pain are seen in the lives of Joni Eareckson and the apostle Paul.

Joni, the young woman who has been a quadriplegic since a diving accident in 1967, has grown through her pain in miraculous ways. Her books, videotapes, and paintings are all results of her struggle to meet pain face-to-face as she grows closer to the Lord and ministers to others with similar needs.

The apostle Paul experienced the pain of beatings, imprisonment, and poor eyesight, to name just a few of his adversities. If anyone had an excuse to give up, he certainly did.

But he didn't. Instead Paul grew through his pain and turned it into a blessing. From the pain of prison he witnessed to his guards. From his jail cell he wrote letters of encouragement and hope to his fellow believers. Through Paul's pain, countless Christians grew in their faith and knowledge of Christ. Thank God for pain!

Life without pain would be life without challenge. When pain attacks our lives, we can either curl up beneath the hurt or rise up to meet the challenge. What challenge? The challenge to be productive, to conquer the odds, and to find the positive in the midst of the negative.

Tom Jackson is a man who meets the challenges of life head-on. For many years his wife, Betty, suffered from a rare debilitating disease that affected not only her body but her mind as well. Eventually her condition required constant medical care and Tom admitted her to a nursing home.

Everyday Tom visited Betty, took her for walks, fed her, and took care of her various needs. As her condition gradually worsened, Betty often failed to recognize the most familiar faces, even the face of her husband.

The daily experience of seeing his beloved wife suffer at the hands of such a merciless disease surely gave new meaning to the word *pain.* Yet Tom Jackson accepted the pain and its subsequent challenge and searched until he found a positive side to his suffering.

One day, after updating me on his wife's condition, Tom said, "You know, I am truly blessed. Many people who visit their loved ones in nursing homes get chewed out for not coming to visit often enough or staying long enough. But I'm lucky. Betty may not always recognize me, but she's happy and content. I'm blessed for that."

For a moment I was speechless as I marveled at such a positive perspective on pain. Truly I was in the presence of one who accepted pain as a part of life and had learned to really live.

Thank God for pain.

13

Don't Sweat the Small Stuff

Nap time was always an interesting, sometimes exasperating experience at the Happy Hearts Day-Care Center, especially in Louise's room. Convincing fourteen four-year-olds to lie quietly on their cots until they went to sleep was quite a task. But on one particular Monday, the job was even more difficult because of Jeffrey.

Jeffrey had arrived that morning sporting shiny new cowboy boots. He proudly strutted around the room giving every child the privilege and opportunity to ooh and aah. Louise wondered why Jeffrey appeared much calmer than usual until she realized that he was simply protecting his new boots from scuffs or scars. *Those boots are a blessing in disguise,* Louise thought to herself. At least, that's what she thought until nap time.

Immediately after lunch the children reluctantly took off their shoes, placed them under their cots, and settled down for a few hours sleep—all except for Jeffrey who lay on his cot staring contentedly down at his boots which he still wore.

"Jeffrey, let me help you get your boots off," Louise whispered.

"No," came the firm reply. "I'm going to leave them on."

"But you know we don't sleep with our shoes on . . . or our boots," Louise persisted. "See. All of the other children have their shoes off."

"I don't care," Jeffrey stubbornly declared. "I'm keeping my boots on."

So the argument continued until Louise was out of patience, Jeffrey was in tears, and the thirteen other children were wide awake wondering who would win the battle.

The battle was finally resolved when Louise stopped reciting the child-care manual and asked herself, "What difference does it make? What's the harm in letting a little four-year-old boy sleep with his new boots on? Who cares anyway?"

Thirty minutes later Louise surveyed her children. The class of four-year-olds was quietly resting, including Jeffrey who occasionally reached down to stroke the new boots he still wore.

Small stuff. Those little occurrences that so easily get under our skin—traffic jams, a customer ahead of you in the express lane with at least twenty items, a flat tire, a broken fingernail, a malfunctioning computer, or someone who refuses to abide by the rules—like Jeffrey.

What it boils down to is that many things that get our dander up and make our blood pressures rise aren't worth the energy we expend over them. In the overall scheme of life, what difference does it make? When all is said and done, will the traffic jams and inconsiderate people really affect the outcome of our lives unless we allow them to?

The next time you feel your blood pressure rising and your temper surfacing, stop and determine whether or not the situation is small stuff. Ask yourself:

- Will this affect someone's physical or spiritual well-being?
- Will it affect someone's sense of self-worth?
- Will this situation affect someone's safety or reputation?

You'll be surprised at how many situations are really small stuff. But while a situation may be small stuff, our response to it can have an incredible impact on our lives.

Take Randy, for example. Randy played on his church's volleyball team and was known for being rude, hot tempered, and a sore loser on the court. Why? Because of his response to the sport.

Randy couldn't stand to lose a point, much less a game. Yet in all honesty, the volleyball games were really pretty small stuff. In and of itself, a game did not affect Randy's spiritual well-being, his sense of self-worth, his safety, or his reputation.

Randy's response to a game, however, made an incredible impact on his life. Whereas the sport should have been beneficial to his health, it only drove his blood pressure through the roof. Spiritually, he destroyed his effectiveness as a Christian witness, and his reputation was such that no one wanted to play on his team. Randy even chose to determine his self-worth based on the outcome of the game. All of this happened because of a net, two poles, and a white ball.

What ranks on your list of small stuff? A sport? Traffic jams? Rude people? A run in your hose or a stain on your favorite tie? Receiving your steak medium rare when you ordered well done? A cranky individual who's impossible to please? Rainy days, sunny days, hot days, cold days? Go ahead. Add your all-time favorite to the list. It's only small stuff._____

Small stuff—it's just not worth the time and effort we give it. My husband helped me learn this lesson late one evening as I bemoaned the fact that the house was still a wreck, the supper dishes still lined the kitchen counter, and I'd only made a small dent in the laundry that day.

After listening to my song and dance for a minute, Scott looked at me and said, "Is that what you want your epitaph to say: 'She was a good housekeeper'?"

He was right. I'd rather be remembered for being a loving, gentle lady who genuinely desired to be like her Savior. Everything else is really pretty small stuff.

14

Leaning Ladders

Jennifer was my best friend throughout high school and college. We were like Mutt and Jeff, as different as daylight and dark. Jennifer was tall—like a model. I was—and still am—relatively short. She drove a brand-new sports car. I drove a fourteen-year-old Ford Falcon. Jennifer was from a Catholic background. I was a Baptist preacher's kid.

I've never been quite sure what brought us together, unless it was our love for music. But regardless of the reason, ours was a unique and very special friendship.

After college Jennifer and I continued to lead vastly divergent lives. She lived the fast-paced, glamorous life-style of a single and worked as a high-ranking executive secretary. I, on the other hand, married a minister, worked as a free-lance writer, and had two babies. Yet through the years we've kept up with each other, especially on birthdays.

Birthdays were always special times of celebration for us in high school and college. And since my birthday is two months before Jennifer's I thoroughly enjoyed being the first one to turn sixteen, eighteen, and twenty-one. For two full months I could boast that I had arrived at those magical milestones ahead of Jennifer.

The boasting has long since ceased, however, as the years have passed. One day I called Jennifer on her thirtieth birthday to offer my sympathies and consolation. I assured her that I was two months ahead of her and still living a happy, productive life. *Thirty* was not deadly, no matter what anyone said.

Toward the end of our conversation, Jennifer asked about my family and said, "You know, Deanna, I wish I had a family like you do. I miss having someone to share my life with. I never dreamed I'd ever want to be a wife and mother. But now I do."

Jennifer's words were brief, but they hit hard. We'd spent many long hours talking about what we wanted out of life, and society's glamorous portrayal of the swinging single had intrigued my best friend. That's what she wanted and that's what she'd set out to seize and secure.

But by the time Jennifer got what she thought she wanted, she realized that society had sold her a pack of lies. She'd climbed her ladder of success to the top, but she didn't like what she found once she arrived.

We all climb ladders throughout life. Our dreams and goals require that we advance over a series of rungs in order to accomplish what we've set out to do. The book store shelves are lined with best-sellers about how to make it to the "top of the heap" and look out for yourself. Book after book tells how to successfully climb your personal ladder.

There's nothing wrong with ladders. We'd have a tough time doing a lot of things without their help. But there's one important point worth noting about ladders. A ladder must lean against something in order for it to be climbed. It either leans against itself, as in the case of a stepladder, or it must be positioned against a secure structure such as a wall or a sturdy tree.

The secret to making it to the top of a ladder lies in the strength of the structure against which it leans. Just as wooden or aluminum ladders lean against structures, so do the ladders of our lives. And just as the key to a good ladder lies in the strength of the structure against which it leans, so the key to climbing successful ladders throughout our lives is found in the strength of the walls we choose for support.

There are many walls available to support our ladders. Some even call out to us . . . making tempting offers . . . promising success. Money, pride, promotion, security, glamour, fame, prestige, romance—they all offer walls of support, at least for awhile. But eventually they begin to crumble and fall.

There is another type of wall which offers strength and support. It is a human wall. Parents, friends, spouse, and children —all freely offer themselves, and to a certain extent they can indeed be towers of strength as we lean upon them.

. But even our friends and loved ones are not strong enough to continually support the ladders of our lives. Nor is it fair to expect or demand them to do so. Many a marriage has collapsed, and many a child has left home in open rebellion due to unfair expectations to be continuous walls of strength.

There is only one wall capable of supporting the ladders of life, and that wall is Jesus Christ. Only He can be counted on to catch us when we start to fall. Only He has the wisdom to guide our steps as we advance from one rung to the next. For only He knows what waits for us at the top.

15

Laughing at Life

It was quite an impressive gathering of ministers and their wives. The event: a whiz-bang summer cookout. The place: our home. The menu: hamburgers with all the trimmings followed by my specialty dessert: banana pudding.

The evening was a great success. Everything went smoothly, and I got rave reviews on my pudding. One man commented that normally he didn't like banana pudding but mine had a special flare. He even had a second hefty helping.

After everyone went home that night my husband had another serving of pudding. "You know, Deanna," he said between mouthfuls, "it tastes lemony. That's the difference. Did you use lemon pudding?"

"Of course not! Whoever heard of using lemon pudding to make banana pudding? That's absurd. I made it according to the same recipe I've always used."

Nevertheless I had to agree. The banana pudding definitely tasted lemony. So much so that I dug through the trash bag until I found the empty pudding boxes.

"See, I knew I used vanilla pudding, just like always."

"Well, it still tastes lemony."

"Maybe the pudding people mismarked the boxes. That's it! I'll put the blame on a factory slipup."

With that temporary explanation we left the pudding behind

us and went to bed. The mystery was solved the next day when I unloaded the dishwasher. A strange looking film was all over the "clean" dishes. It was soap . . . lemon-scented soap!

An immediate investigation revealed that the rinse cycle on the dishwasher had not functioned. Quickly I recounted the previous load of dirty dishes. Sure enough! The bowl that held the banana pudding had come straight out of the dishwasher, lemon film and all.

Oh how awful! How disgusting! How embarrassing! I'd fed my unsuspecting guests soap pudding! But what could I do about it? Nothing! Nothing except throw out the remaining pudding, call the repairman, pray that no one got sick, and laugh.

The lemon-banana pudding is not the only kitchen catastrophe I've had. There've been many—like the time I made banana-nut bread and the dough was too thick. It was so thick, in fact, that it was impossible to mix. It just clung to the spatula in one big glob. The beaters could not even turn through it.

Before long I was exhausted and exasperated. Nothing like that had ever happened before, and I'd made that same recipe dozens of times. But the harder I tried the worse it got—until I finally discovered the problem.

The problem was one ingredient I'd omitted—the *bananas*. Leave it to me to attempt to make banana-nut bread without bananas. Julia Child I'm not. There was only one thing to do. Add the missing ingredient and laugh.

Why laugh? Because laughter relieves tension. Too many times we get all wound up over events that are really just simple mistakes. You know: bloopers and blunders like tripping across a platform in front of hundreds of people, arriving late for a meeting and discovering the only empty chair is on the front row, spilling coffee on your boss, or showing up at work dressed in two different colored shoes, neither of which matches your outfit.

Why laugh? Because laughter helps keep things in perspective. Laughter keeps molehills from escalating into mountains. It keeps mild skirmishes from developing into all-out wars. It keeps petty concerns from expanding into ulcer-causing worry. It helps keep life on an even keel.

Erma Bombeck, newspaper columnist and author of many humorous books, once received a letter from a young mother who was serving time in prison because she had killed her child. After reading humorous stories about mothers and motherhood the woman wrote Erma and said, "Had I known mothers could laugh at those things, I probably wouldn't be where I am today."[1]

Laughter: it helps keep things in perspective. It prevents us from taking the everyday occurrences of life too seriously.

Laughter also has a unique healing power. It has the ability to smooth ruffled feathers, mend hurting hearts, and brighten even the gloomiest day.

Not only does laughter affect us emotionally and mentally, it also has positive physical effects. Explosive guffaws, cackles, and roars have been proven to provide excellent exercise for muscles in the face, arms, legs, chest, and stomach. They are even capable of reducing stress. Experts believe that because laughter releases pain-killing chemicals produced by the brain, it has the ability to relieve minor aches and pains.

So go ahead. Let out a good guffaw. Lose control and allow your giggle box to tip on over. It will be good for you, in more ways than one.

The writer of Proverbs said it this way: "A cheerful heart is good medicine,/but a crushed spirit dries up the bones" (17:22).

How are your bones? Are they brittle and dry? Do you sound

like a skeleton when you walk? If so, you need a good dose of laughter.

Take a dose of laughter. Read the comics or watch a funny movie.

Take a dose of laughter. Practice laughing aloud when other people laugh.

Take a dose of laughter. Laugh at your own bloopers and blunders and laugh with other people when they make the same foolish mistakes.

Take a dose of laughter. Laugh at the silly situations life hands you. Throw your head back, lose control, and cackle until the tears flow. After all, you'll only be taking your own medicine.

Note

1. Erma Bombeck, *Motherhood: The Second Oldest Profession,* (New York: McGraw-Hill Book Company, 1983), p. 3.

16

He Maketh Me to Lie Down

There is an enemy in our midst that threatens our health, happiness, and spiritual well-being. It wears many creative masks in order to trap and deceive us—its victims.

The enemy rarely attacks head-on. Instead it quietly creeps up and saps our strength from behind and within. Before we're even aware of its presence, it has launched a vicious attack on our bodies and souls, and we've lost the battle before it begins.

The enemy? Fatigue.

Several years ago a young minister was asked to pastor a new church located in the middle of a rapidly growing suburb. In just a matter of months, the small congregation outgrew its original facilities as the pastor's dynamic personality and evangelistic messages attracted new members from every area of the city. The people enthusiastically launched building programs and various new plans of ministry. An attitude of "nothing can stop us now" prevailed.

But something did stop them. At least, something stopped one of them. One morning, the young pastor could not wake up. No matter how hard he tried he simply could not shake the cobwebs from his head, nor could he manage to get out of bed. Fatigue had sapped the energetic minister of all his strength. The enemy had won the battle.

Another classic example of fatigue is recorded in 1 Kings

19:1-8. Queen Jezebel had put out a death warrant on the prophet Elijah that sent him running for his life. Finally, in utter exhaustion, Elijah stopped running and prayed that he would die. He'd had enough. It was over. He had no more to give. Fatigue had won the battle decisively.

But let's take a look at the events leading up to 1 Kings 19. Interestingly enough, Elijah had experienced one success after another. He had challenged the prophets of Baal to a test in order to prove who was the one true God. It was quite a spectacular show of God's power. The prophets of Baal fell in total defeat. Following that victory, Elijah brought about the end of a drought by praying down rain. Another impressive, victorious experience!

Then fatigue set in. Elijah was physically, emotionally, mentally, and spiritually exhausted. Imagine how he might have been treated if he'd had that same experience today. He probably would have heard well-meaning friends say things like, "Pick yourself up. You've got to keep on going. There's so much left to be done."

"Look at your past victories. You've no reason to feel depressed."

"What do you mean you want to die? That's ridiculous!"

"Think positively! You must believe." And so on, and so on, and so on.

God, however, did not bless Elijah with pep talks or pats on the back. No, God allowed Elijah to rest. Not a catnap to keep him going for a few more hours but a complete rest to refresh his body and soul.

First Kings 19:5-8 says that Elijah slept and when he awoke an angel was there with food and water. After eating Elijah went back to sleep, and a second time he awoke and found the angel with his supper already prepared. This time the angel said, "Get up and eat, for the journey is too much for you" (v. 7).

That's the key right there. The journey of life is too much for any of us to bear without proper rest and nourishment. God, in His infinite wisdom, knew that we would have a difficult time accepting this fact. And so He *commanded* us to rest. At least five times throughout the Book of Exodus alone, God commanded His people to rest in order to be refreshed.

In the New Testament we read where Christ was concerned for His disciples' overall well-being. On a day when so many people clamored about them that they didn't even have time to eat, Christ finally told His disciples to get away by themselves. He instructed them to find a quiet place where they could get some rest. (See Mark 6:31.)

The angel was right. The journey of life is too much for us to bear without rest. Without it, fatigue is inevitable.

Think about some of the characteristics of fatigue: baggy eyes, loss of energy, inability to think straight or keep things in proper perspective, lack of motivation, irritability, and depression. Not a pretty picture, is it? No wonder God orders us to rest. There's no way we can live effective, productive Christian lives when we suffer from chronic fatigue.

The ironic part of our current way of thinking among Christian circles is that bloodshot, baggy eyes and lack of sleep are signs of spirituality. Unless persons are constantly running to and fro from one Christian activity to another until they drop dead in their tracks, they are not perceived as being very spiritual.

Hold it! Wait just a minute! Let's make a quick review of the twenty-third Psalm. Verse 2 says that God "*makes* me lie down in green pastures." He's serious about resting our tired bodies, minds, and spirits.

Notice where God makes us rest—not in a briar patch but

in green pastures. Imagine lying in a thick, green, luscious lawn on a fresh spring day with the warmth of the sun's rays caressing your skin. Now that's restful! And that is *God's* idea of rest. Green pastures, cool streams, restoration for the soul—that's what God *wants* for us.

While some zealous go-getters may reprimand you for seeking rest, remember this. On more than one occasion Christ left the crowds behind and went off alone—to rest. Sometimes He let His disciples tag along, while other times He sought complete solitude. Then, after a period of rest, Christ returned to the hustle and bustle of life, refreshed and ready to meet the demands of His life's journey.

Surely if Christ, who was fully human yet fully divine, was willing to admit His human limitations, then we, in our complete humanness need to acknowledge our need for rest. God, in His mercy, has commanded it and provided for it. Let's wise up and gratefully accept it! Only then will we be able to continue life's journey.

17

Paying the Price

The most recent issue of *Writer's Digest* arrived in the mail today. Being a writer, I feel it is my duty to subscribe to the magazine. It makes me look professional. It is also tax deductible.

Seriously, when it arrived I thumbed through the pages and came across this observation. Most writers, according to one observant soul, want to have written a book. They don't necessarily want to write a book: they want *to have written* a book.

How true, how true! Many writers want the finished product without paying the price. They want to have autograph parties and appear on television talk shows, but they really don't want to put in the long hours of writing, rewriting, and rewriting some more. Neither do they want to invest in pens, pencils, paper, a typewriter, and postage stamps.

Does that sound just a little bit familiar? Oh, you may not be a writer, but have you ever wanted something without wanting to pay the price? For example:

• Many lackadaisical people want to be in excellent physical condition, but they don't want to exercise.

• Many business people want to receive promotions in their jobs, but they don't want to meet the necessary requirements.

• Most of us want to lose weight at one time or another, but we don't want to cut back on how much we eat.

• Lots of folks want to have friends, but they don't want to make the effort to be a friend.

• Many Americans want to live in a free nation, but they don't exercise their freedom to vote.

• Countless loan applicants want to have more money, but they don't want to manage what money they have by living on a budget.

• The nation's high schools are filled with students who want the benefits of a high school diploma and a college degree, but they don't want to spend much time studying.

If you fall into one of these categories, don't worry. You're not alone. There are even those of us who at one time or another dreamed of being concert musicians or professional athletes. But we never seemed to find much time to practice.

It all goes back to "No pain, no gain" and "No guts, no glory." There's a price to be paid for the things we want in life. That goes for spiritual things, too.

There is a price to be paid if we want to really know Jesus Christ on a personal level. It costs us to have the privilege of serving Him. A price must be paid if we want a close relationship with our Heavenly Father. The question is whether or not we're willing to pay it.

Nathan the prophet was willing to pay the price. He risked his life in order to deliver a blood-chilling message from God to King David.

Joseph was willing to pay the price. He spent time in an Egyptian prison in order to serve his God.

Daniel was willing to pay the price. He spent the night with a den full of hungry lions because he refused to stop praying.

Stephen was willing to pay the price. He preached the gospel of Christ even though it meant his imminent death.

The price to know and serve God is great. It often varies from one individual to another. God may ask one believer to sacrifice wealth in order to serve Him while He asks another to give up fame. One believer may be required to endure years of tedious education while another is asked to give up the comforts and security of home.

For one young man the price was incredibly high. His own desire was to pastor a small country church, but that was not what God had planned.

At the age of thirty, the young minister became famous while preaching in Los Angeles. And that was just the beginning. God's plan was for his ministry to grow until it spread across the entire United States and eventually around the world.

But there was a price to be paid in order to serve God as He directed. And the price was tremendously high, for the young preacher had to sacrifice his cherished time with his wife and children.

While he traveled around the world, sharing the gospel with more people than any other individual, the minister's family stayed behind. In his absence they lived and loved and learned. They shared special moments that could never be experienced through letters or phone calls. The minister's entire family paid quite a high price in order to serve their Lord.

Long ago the name of this dynamic man became a household word. His name is Billy Graham. Often I've looked at him and other great Christian leaders and thought, *Wow, I wish I had their faith . . . their knowledge . . . their spiritual maturity.*

And then I'm reminded of the price that was paid: countless hours of Bible study, a lifetime spent in the presence of God through soul-searching prayer, a humble dedicated spirit of service, a willingness to sacrifice personal desires, normal family life, and sometimes even personal safety.

No, the life of a dynamic servant of God does not just evolve over the course of time. A price is always paid.

What price is God asking you to pay? What sacrifice is He

asking you to make? Where do you stand in the struggle to obediently follow Him?

Whatever sacrifice God asks us to make, we can know without doubt that it's worth the price in order to have a right relationship with Him.

God understands what sacrifice is all about. After all, He sacrificed the life of His only Son in order that we might have a relationship with Him. Surely we can rest in the knowledge that though He asks us to make sacrifices, He will make it well worth our while.

18

The Elusive Thing Called Time

Hanging on my bedroom wall is one of those picture frames that displays about two dozen snapshots of various sizes. The conglomeration depicts events ranging from my wedding to Christmas to building a snowman.

One picture in particular, however, has a strange effect on me whenever I look at it. The person in the picture is a bright young woman with sparkling eyes and a brilliant smile that defies pessimism and defeat. It's a picture of me as I walked down the aisle at my college graduation.

Every time I see that picture I'm reminded that time waits for no one. It marches steadily on, with or without our consent. It seems like it was only yesterday that I considered my options as a college graduate and made some crucial decisions. But it wasn't yesterday. It was many years ago.

What has happened since that picture was taken? Time has passed, and life has been lived. That's it in a nutshell.

The critical question we must all answer is: "What is being accomplished as we live our lives?" Obviously we are busy doing something. We rush through our lives at breakneck speed. It would take a small miracle to squeeze anything else into our ridiculously hectic schedules. And the amazing thing is that while you feel your life is busier than anyone else's, *we all* feel that way about our lives.

Why are we so busy? Why are our lives so frenzied? Where are we headed?

The story has been told about a policeman who stopped a woman for speeding and asked her where she was going. "I don't know," she replied, "but I'm getting there as fast as I can!"

We may be getting there as fast as we can, but where exactly is *there*? Where are we headed? What are we accomplishing along the way? And what are we planning to do once we get there?

Maybe we need to take a few precious moments of our time and evaluate where we stand. First, write down a brief description of how you live your life. Consider how you spend the hours of your days. What are you accomplishing?

_____

_____

Next, write down what you believe God wants you to accomplish with your time. Be as specific as possible.

_____

_____

How does the description of your life as you live it now compare to what you believe God wants you to be doing?

_____

_____

Now, how do you need to be spending your time in order to accomplish what God wants you to do? Again, be specific.

_____

_____

There are no magic formulas to increase the number of hours in our days. The key is to use each irretrievable minute wisely.

While there are many excellent books available on time management, there is one simple suggestion that seems to work well.

Begin each day by praying, "Lord, how do You want me to use the minutes and hours that lie before me today? I dedicate each one to You, and I ask that You grant me wisdom to use them wisely. Help me to resist the temptation to spend my time as other people tell me I should. Instead, please give me the courage to use my day as *You* guide and direct each step."

Having begun your day with that prayer, go about your daily tasks with the calm awareness that your time is in the Lord's hands. But be on guard for this: whenever we turn our hectic schedules over to the Lord, He may very well begin making alterations. Be ready to change, rearrange, add, and delete.

Recently I picked up a newspaper and was shocked to read that an acquaintance, a young woman in her mid-twenties, had died in a car accident. Once again I was reminded that time waits for no one. Youth or good health is no guarantee of tomorrow. Time marches on with no regard for our individual plans and preferences.

Now is the time to begin using our minutes and hours wisely. Not at a hectic, sanity-threatening pace, attempting to fill every waking moment with constant activity. But it's time to start living life at whatever pace God sets for you.

Now is the time to commit those elusive hours and minutes to the Lord. Then, whenever someone or something reminds you of years passed, you can know with confidence that the time was not spent spinning your wheels as you hurried from one event to the next. Rather your time was spent wisely and productively, living for the Lord.

19

The Significant Small

One crisp autumn morning, many years ago, an elderly gentleman made his way to a local department store. After locating the greeting card display he stood for several minutes before the section marked "Birthday." Carefully, pensively he studied the selection. This was no time to hurry. His youngest granddaughter was going to be one year old on Friday. Her first birthday card from her Poppie had to be special.

It seemed silly to put so much time and effort into selecting a card for a little girl who couldn't talk or read. Why, she'd probably be more interested in the envelope than the card. She certainly wouldn't understand its message. Nevertheless, he continued the search until he found just the right one.

After making his purchase he returned home where he sat down and wrote a brief note. If the card was special, his words had to be even more so. Slowly, meticulously he chose the words to express his love and affection. Once that was done, he addressed the envelope and set the sealed card aside to await the next day's mail.

Over twenty years passed, yet my birthday card from my grandfather never arrived. For some reason it was never mailed. But then one day while visiting my grandmother, she handed me an old, yellowed envelope. She'd found it on the floor of her closet a few days earlier, she explained. She had no idea how it had gotten there.

Curious, I turned the envelope over and discovered that it was addressed to me in my grandfather's handwriting. Gently I pulled out the fragile card and read "Happy Birthday One-Year-Old." The baby-blue design had faded with age but the message written by Poppie was still crystal clear.

My grandfather, who had passed away many years earlier, could never have imagined the joy that his simple selection would bring me. Why, it was just a birthday card. How much significance could a card hold?

How many times have you asked yourself that same question? "How could that little deed possibly hold any meaning? What difference would it make?" Our efforts often seem so simple, so insignificant that it's tempting to leave them undone. But small, simple deeds often make the most impact on the lives of other people. Think, for example, how many times you've wanted someone to:

- listen to your concern without offering cold counsel;
- call, anyone to call, in order to break the monotony of a lonely evening;
- pay you a compliment, proving that your hard work was appreciated by at least one individual;
- remember a sad occasion such as the anniversary of the death of a loved one;
- bring a meal to your home when you've had the flu;
- give you a firm hug around the shoulders when life has been painfully unkind.
- remember a special occasion such as your birthday or an anniversary.

The list can be as long as you want to make it. Remember, if these are things that would brighten your day you can safely assume that they would brighten someone else's life, too.

Sometimes, however, small deeds do more than just brighten someone's day. They can plant seeds, open doors, and pave the way for the future. One mother brightened her son's day by giving him her old green coat to play with. But she not only brightened his day, she unknowingly opened the door to his future. For with that old green coat the boy made a puppet . . . his first puppet. The boy's name was Jim Henson, the creator of Big Bird, Kermit the Frog, Miss Piggy, Bert and Ernie, and the rest of the captivating Muppets.

Another parent brightened his son's night when he woke him up and drove to a meadow where they watched a meteor shower. But was that really significant in the boy's life? Apparently so. The six-year-old boy was Steven Spielberg who says that the meteor shower was the seed which, many years later, grew into his box-office hit: *Close Encounters of the Third Kind.*

Small deeds: those seemingly insignificant acts that appear so small next to major gestures and accomplishments that the whole world sees, yet often have the greatest impact.

William Wordsworth once said that the best part of a person's life is the "little, nameless, unremembered acts of kindness and of love." And the great preacher Peter Marshall once said, "Small deeds done are better than great deeds planned."

So go ahead and carry out a small deed while you plan a big one. Make a phone call instead of waiting to visit a friend. Meet your new neighbors even though you don't have a house-warming gift. Send a card even though a letter might be better. A signed card is better than an unwritten letter any day. It may not seem like much to you, but you never know what impact it may have. Your efforts may seem small, but they are not insignificant.

20

In Search of the American Dream

One warm summer evening, several years ago, my husband strapped our eight-month-old daughter into her stroller and announced, "We're going out to pull weeds." With that farewell the twosome headed out to the yard for one of their many father-daughter discussions.

After talking awhile about grass, flowers, trees, and other bits of nature Scott began to wax philosophical.

"Melanie," he began, "some day, when you're all grown up, you're going to meet a handsome guy—just like your mommy did. And the two of you are going to fall madly in love and get married. *Then*," he continued, "you're going to work hard, save all of your money, and buy a house. And *then* you're going to continue working very hard, so you can spend all of your money buying bags of fertilizer which you will take home and throw on the ground. This, Melanie, is what is known as the American dream."

The American dream: that tempting seductress which says that every American should own this or that material possession in order to be happy and fulfilled. For some it's a house and two cars. For others it's boats, vacation homes, or swimming pools.

That's not all. Once you own the basic necessities of the American dream—whatever you consider them to be—there are all of the other toys and trinkets that advertisers say we must have. One major computer company ran a television ad which implied that a child would be unattractive, overweight, and well below average if he or she did not have a home computer.

Other advertisers try to convince us that we simply must possess their products such as videocassette recorders, microwave ovens, designer clothes, video games, solid-wood furniture, and membership at the new health club. The list goes on and on. The tragedy is that it has no end.

Not long ago I heard of a couple who had clearly been seduced by the American dream. Tom and Pam were in their mid-thirties when things started looking up. Tom's promotion along with Pam's income made it possible for them to sell their modest home and buy a large two-story mansion complete with swimming pool, tennis court, and live-in servants.

That was only the beginning. Next came two new foreign sports cars, a boat, and complete new wardrobes for every member of their family. This was the dream they had searched for, longed for, and worked for. Finally it had come true and they planned to enjoy it to the fullest.

Tom and Pam's dream suddenly turned into a nightmare when Tom's company fell to bad economic conditions and was forced to declare bankruptcy. The house, the cars, the boat—everything was lost in a matter of weeks as they watched the American dream slip through their fingers.

Most of us are like Tom and Pam. Oh, we probably don't have to worry about sudden financial good fortune, but we must face the same questions concerning the money we possess and how we choose to use it. We must each one answer the crucial question: "How do I, as a follower of Christ, juggle the American dream with my spiritual life?"

Are Christians supposed to shun all material possessions and luxuries? Is it wrong to enjoy nice houses, cars, and clothes? As is true in many areas of life, one vitally important factor is our attitude toward pursuing the American dream. Are our goals and desires in line with Christ's teachings and principles? Let's make a quick attitude check and see what happens.

1. Is there any material item that you sincerely want? For example, every time you go into a store do you wander by a specific item and dream of owning it? If so, what is it?

2. Is there something that you want but simply cannot afford? If so, name it.

3. Do you feel frustrated or angry because you cannot have a particular possession?

4. Do you feel unhappy every time you think about what you do not have?

5. Do you spend numerous hours trying to devise a scheme whereby you could obtain a particular possession?

6. Are you ever tempted to give less to the Lord and His work in order to save more toward making a purchase?

7. Do you envy other people who have what you want but cannot afford?

8. Are you in debt up to your ears in pursuit of the American dream?

How did you do? Do you have your "want list" in proper perspective, or are you struggling with feelings of envy and frustration? Psalm 49:16-17 says, "Do not be overawed when a man grows rich,/when the splendor of his house increases;/ for he will take nothing with him when he dies."

To put it another way, you can't take it with you. To which comes the reply, "I don't want to take it with me. I just want to enjoy it down here on earth." Ah, there's the rub. Exactly how can we enjoy the good things of life on earth?

Christ's advice is to "Seek his kingdom, and these things will be given to you as well," (Luke 12:31). What things? Our needs, all of our needs. He doesn't promise to provide for all of our wants, but when we seek His kingdom first, before our desires, it's amazing what happens to our perspective on material things.

What about the possessions God so richly bestows upon us? What should our attitude be toward them? Albert Schweitzer summed it up when he said, "If you own something that you cannot give away, you don't own it. It owns you."

21

Putting the Pieces Together

Working a jigsaw puzzle is a paradoxical activity. In a matter of minutes a puzzle worker can experience numerous emotions ranging from relaxation and enjoyment to frustration and stress. And what is the cause of this wide range of emotions? One tiny piece of oddly shaped cardboard.

Consider a piece of a jigsaw puzzle. Any piece will do. It may have one or two flat sides or numerous protrusions. Regardless of its appearance, however, there are four qualities that are characteristic of every piece.

First of all, every piece of a puzzle has a unique shape. Some pieces may closely resemble each other but no two pieces of the same puzzle are identical. Each one has its own place. Go ahead. Just try to fit it into the wrong slot. It won't work no matter how hard you try.

Secondly, each piece has a special coloring which gives a clue as to what area of the puzzle it belongs. A major step in working a puzzle is to separate the pieces according to color. But even within specific color piles there are various shades and hues. Each piece is unique.

Next, each piece of a puzzle affects the pieces around it. You'll never see a puzzle that calls for a piece to stand totally alone. Instead, when positioned properly, each piece interlocks with several other pieces to form a significant portion of the puzzle. Those pieces affect other pieces, and so on. In effect, one small piece indirectly touches countless others.

Finally, every piece, no matter how small or oddly shaped, plays a vital role in the overall picture. Imagine the frustration of spending many hours working a puzzle only to discover that one piece is missing. No! It can't be! The puzzle can never be complete without every piece filling its appropriate position, no matter how small it may be. *Every piece is significant.*

So much for the discourse on puzzles. Let's consider you and me. We are very much like pieces of a puzzle. God created each one of us with a special shape, size, and coloring. We each have a specific temperament and intellect. We have various interests and goals that are personally ours. All of these things make us unique creations of God.

The question we must answer is: How do we as unique individuals fit into the puzzle of life? Where do we fit into God's overall plan?

Just as a piece of puzzle affects the pieces around it, we affect the lives of everyone around us. Our lives interlock with the lives of those who are closest to us and then, as their lives interlock with other people's lives, we indirectly touch the lives of countless people who we may not ever know. Imagine the number of people touched throughout the course of a lifetime.

Recently, while preparing to lead a dating/marriage seminar, a friend shared with me something that one of her college professors had told her years ago. She said that her professor believed one of the major causes of marital difficulties was that a Christian marriage is the attempt to create something permanent in a disposable world. In our society, if something is damaged or broken we simple throw it away instead of repairing it.

What a profound thought. That professor's teaching not only became a part of the seminar but it also made me even more sensitive to the needs of my own marriage. I've never met the man, and probably never will. But because his life was at one time interlocked with the life of my friend, whose life is now interlocked with mine, the professor indirectly had a positive impact upon my life.

Perhaps one of the most important lessons we can learn from a jigsaw puzzle is that *every individual life is important.* It takes each one of us to make up the overall picture of God's plan. The problems arise when we decide, for whatever reason, that God made a mistake in how He made us and try to make ourselves into something other than what He intended. We can really mess up the picture when we don't accept ourselves the way God made us.

Paul referred to this idea in his first letter to the believers in Corinth when he wrote about the variety of spiritual gifts given to Christians. In the twelfth chapter he said that there are many gifts and many different kinds of service. And they are all given for the purpose of helping the entire body of believers.

Paul went on to say that no one gift is better than another. Each one has its specific purpose. Now get this: the distribution of gifts is God's choice. Just as He decides the color of our hair and our ultimate height, He also decides what gifts and abilities we should have. It's His choice, and only He knows what is best.

Many years ago I had the privilege of meeting an incredible lady named Susan Ray. One of the things I remember about visiting in the Ray's home is seeing Susan's bedroom. It was beautifully decorated in lavender and white; overall, it was not all that different from other young ladies' rooms. Except for one thing: in place of a white French provincial bed stood a polished white iron lung.

In the early 1950s, at the age of four, Susan suffered from paralytic polio. From that point on, she has lived her days in a reclining wheelchair and her nights in an iron lung. But somewhere along the road, Susan decided that she was indeed "fearfully and wonderfully made" (Ps. 139:14). With the help of her family she graduated from college, works as a writer, and paints. All the while Susan's life interlocks with people around her, completing her corner of the puzzle.

God, in His infinite wisdom, has made each of us unique pieces of His puzzle. The same God who created the universe gave us each a place to belong. He's the only one who sees the complete picture, however, and we must believe that He knew what He was doing when He created us to fit into His plan. It's only when we accept ourselves as He made us that the puzzle will ever fit together and the picture be complete.

22

Creative Giving

I've always been a gift giver. Christmas, birthdays, anniversaries, Valentine's Day, Groundhog Day, Support-Your-Local-Police-Department Day. Give me any reason to celebrate and I'll jump at the chance to buy a special card or prepare a favorite meal.

Of course, there are the "just-because" gifts: gifts like cards, flowers, a batch of homemade cookies, or a trinket that holds special meaning. The little gifts that say, "You're special, and I want you to have this . . . just because."

Giving gifts is not just enjoyable, it's downright fun. Few things bring me more joy than surprising family and friends with small, sometimes nonsensical remembrances. Perhaps that's why a newspaper jewelry advertisement caught my eye one day. The picture was of an eighteen-karat gold bracelet designed by Cartier. The copy beneath it said, "The famous Love Bracelet, for her or for him. The ultimate gift of true love: $1,500.00."

Forgive me, Cartier, but I have to disagree. If a fifteen-hundred-dollar piece of jewelry is the ultimate gift of true love, then a lot of us are in deep trouble.

The truth is: a fifteen-hundred-dollar gold bracelet has nothing to do with genuine giving. Giving has nothing to do with money. Oh, money may be used to purchase a gift, or it may even be the gift itself. But giving involves much, much more.

True giving involves a loving attitude and a sacrificial spirit. Sincerity, creativity, and sensitivity are also key factors. But all too often we place undue emphasis upon the price tag.

Recently, while watching an episode of the television series "M*A*S*H," I was reminded of how society views the act of giving. On this particular episode, it was December in Korea and everyone at the military camp was donating food for the local orphans' Christmas party. Major Charles Emerson Winchester III, a wealthy doctor from a prominent Boston family, contributed a tin of smoked oysters. When questioned about the practicality of his gift he replied, "It's not the size of the gift that matters: it's the cost."

It's sad, but we often fall into society's trap of measuring gifts by dollar signs. We wonder whether the gifts we give friends cost as much as the ones they gave us. If we happen to purchase a present from a discount store, we go to great lengths to remove the evidence, hoping that the friend doesn't ask us where it came from.

How silly can we get? When will we learn the secret to true giving? Some helpful insights can be gained simply by talking to mothers. Ask any mother. She will tell you that the gifts she treasures the most are the ones her children made for her when they were young. You know: the bookmarker, pot holder, and plaster imprint of tiny hands. Even the first attempts at finger painting are priceless because along with the picture came the proud announcement, "Look, Mommy. I made this for you all by myself!"

The combined monetary value of such simple, unpretentious gifts is probably worth less than one dollar. But to a mother, their value is immeasurable. Why? Because they're gifts of love and creativity. They're gifts of the heart.

Last December I asked the members of my Sunday School department to share about a memorable gift that they'd received at some point in their lives. One girl told about her grandmother's desire to give each of her granddaughters a special gift. After much loving consideration, she took her antique lace tablecloth and used it to make handkerchiefs for each granddaughter to carry in her wedding. The gifts cost no money, but the handkerchiefs are priceless because they were gifts of the heart. That grandmother knew what it meant to be a creative giver.

My own grandmother was another creative giver. But she had a problem with numbers. There were so many of us grandchildren and great grandchildren that she could not afford to buy each one of us a gift. But she simply refused to be cheated out of the joy of giving. When there was no money left to buy gifts, she began giving away her own possessions. One of my most cherished treasures is her 1903 edition of *Rebecca of Sunnybrook Farm* that she gave me one Christmas. The gift cost no money, just a creative, loving, and giving heart.

This is the kind of giving that caught Christ's attention. Large monetary values never seemed to impress Him. He looked for something else in a gift. He looked at the condition of the heart. In His estimation, the two small copper coins that the widow gave to the Temple treasury were worth far more than the large amounts given by the rich folks (see Mark 12:41-44).

If Christ was not impressed with showy gifts, why are we? Perhaps it's because we listen to society rather than learning from the example of our Lord. Christ never asked us to see how much we could spend on each other every time a birthday or Christmas rolled around. He asked us to give something far more precious than money. Christ asked us to give of ourselves.

Learning to give of ourselves is the key to genuine giving.

When we give of ourselves, it doesn't matter if there is or isn't any money to purchase a gift. For when we give of ourselves, unselfish creativity takes over and the act of giving discovers a whole new meaning of sincerity and sacrifice.

23

Plants, People, and Other Tools of God

Since the days of Moses God's people have doubted their ability to be used by Him.

Moses argued with God until he was blue in the face. "I'm just a man. No one will believe You sent me. No one will listen to me. And besides, I can't even talk very well!"

Then there was Jeremiah. He argued that he was too young to be God's spokesman (1:6).

Sarah believed she was too old to bear a child. She laughed at the thought of giving Abraham a son in their old age (Gen. 18:12).

Zechariah did not believe that he and his wife, Elizabeth, could have a son, regardless of what the angel said (Luke 1:18).

And so it goes. God's people continue to ask: "Can He really use me? But I'm not witty . . . bright . . . charming . . . beautiful . . . intelligent . . . or talented." On and on the list goes as we fill in the blanks with our own feeble excuses explaining why God can't use us.

Instead of focusing on our human limitations, however, let's take a look at just who God has used in the past. Not only that, let's consider *what* God has used. He not only uses people, He uses things, too.

First, let's peer back into the Old Testament at King David: a mighty warrior, to be sure. And king of Israel! But he also committed adultery and murder. Yet he is one of the most prominent individuals in all of history, for he repented and was forgiven.

God used David in such mighty ways that he stands head and shoulders above the other ancestors of Christ. Christ is even referred to throughout Scripture as the son of David rather than the son of Abraham or the son of Jacob.

Then there was Rahab, the prostitute of Jericho. God used her to hide two Israelite spies when their lives were endangered. Eventually, she was responsible for their successful escape (see Josh. 2:1-15).

What about Saul of Tarsus? He went on an all-out campaign to execute the early Christians. In fact, he was on his way to arrest the believers in Damascus when God grabbed hold of his life (Acts 9:1-3). Just look what happened then!

Still not convinced that God can use you? All right, then, let's look at some inanimate objects for a moment. Objects like plants (Jonah 4:6), a staff (Ex. 4:2), a jawbone (Judg. 15:15), a smooth stone (1 Sam. 17:40), flour and oil (1 Kings 17:12), a tiny cloud (1 Kings 18:44), a mustard seed (Matt. 13:31), and five small loaves of bread along with two scrawny fish (John 6:9).

God chose to use a plant to provide shade for Jonah and ease his discomfort. He used a staff to convince Moses of His power, and with the jawbone of a donkey He empowered Samson to kill a thousand men. It only took one of David's five smooth stones to kill the giant Goliath, and a never-ending supply of flour and oil kept the prophet Elijah alive. Later, one tiny cloud brought about the beginning of the end to a severe drought when Elijah prayed for rain.

The list continues in the New Testament where Christ used inanimate objects in His ministry. In a parable He used a mustard seed to explain a truth concerning the kingdom of heaven.

Perhaps best known are the five loaves of bread and two fish which Christ used to feed over five thousand people. Over and over, seemingly insignificant objects were used to accomplish divine purposes.

Now pardon me for being so bold, but we are made in the image of God Himself. He breathed into us His own spirit of life. Surely if He can use the jawbone of an ass or a loaf of bread, He can use you and me: failures, faults, and all.

God *can* use you and me, but there seem to be two keys to being used by Him. The first is seen in the life of Rahab. Though her life as a prostitute was far from sinless, she had the necessary quality: she was *willing* to let God use her.

That's the first step. We must *want* God to use us. We must be *available* to Him.

But there's another key: to acknowledge God's power. We must quit focusing on our human limitations and focus instead upon His divine strength.

It is God's power, working in and through us, that enables us to accomplish His tasks. It is His power, not our own, that gives us the strength to say, "Yes, Lord. I believe You can use me." We must remember that God chooses to use us "not because of anything we have done but because of his own purpose and grace" (2 Tim. 1:9).

Doug and Donna were two people who didn't think that God could use them. They didn't doubt that God could use other people; they just didn't believe they had any abilities worthy of His time. But they were wrong.

One day, after much thought and prayer, Doug and Donna approached their church's youth minister. "We don't have any special abilities," they began. "All we can really do is cook. But if you can ever use us, we're available. Just let us know."

From that point on Doug and Donna began traveling with their church youth group as the official chefs. Camps, mission trips, choir tours—from one border of the United States to the other. For over ten years they gave up their vacation time each summer in order to keep a bunch of rowdy teenagers well fed and nourished.

If God can use plants and prostitutes, murderers and mustard seeds, then surely He can use you and me. But like everything else God chooses to use, we are powerless to accomplish anything for Him in our own strength. But in *His* strength . . . now that's a different story!

24

The Weary Warrior

David is undoubtedly one of the most colorful characters of all time. His life was spiced with such passion and pageantry that a day without some sort of adventure was surely the exception rather than the rule.

Throughout his life David fulfilled many duties, including the duty of a warrior. From the time he was a shepherd boy and killed the giant Goliath to his unsurpassed military victories, David possessed an astounding power and strength. So great were his conquests that parade goers shouted: "Saul has slain his thousands,/and David his tens of thousands" (1 Sam. 18:7).

But amidst the fanfare and glory there existed another side of David, a side we often fail to see. Take a look at David as he is portrayed in 2 Samuel 21:15-22.

As the story unfolds, David and his men are once again engaged in battle with the Philistines. This time, however, there is not one giant but four. Read the account carefully. It's quite an exciting story. Notice the key phrase in the later part of verse 15. It states that after David fought the battle for awhile "he became exhausted."

Wow! This great, powerful, mighty man of God—a warrior and king—got tired? That's right. He was flat worn out. Verses 16-22 go on to say that David's men fought the remainder of the battle for him. The weary warrior was too tired to go on.

He had to rely on his soldiers to fight the giants and gain the victory. He simply could not continue in the battle.

Our lives are filled with giants. Some live in our homes while others stalk us on our jobs. Still other giants hide their deadly power within our bodies and defiantly rear their ugly heads when least expected. Though we're rarely ready to meet our giants face-to-face, we have no option. They won't go away. Battle is inevitable.

Without question, one of the greatest battles I've ever fought occurred when I taught a high-school "resource" class. Supposedly, the class was for students who had mild learning disabilities, but it was also a last resort for the troublemakers. When other teachers reached their wits end, they transferred the malcontents into the resource class.

For the most part I dealt with the students effectively, all except for Franklin and Ralph. Nothing was new to them. Drugs, alcohol, sex, gang wars, jail—they'd seen it all.

It didn't take long for me to realize that the needs of Franklin and Ralph far exceeded my training. Yet my job was to teach *all* of my students. So day after day I went into the arena to do battle with my giants, and day after day I emerged physically exhausted. Emotionally, I was battered and bruised beyond my wildest imaginings.

As the months wore on, Franklin and Ralph were obviously as determined to see me fail as I was to succeed. Their classroom antics evolved into hostility, and I sensed that they were serious about their threats to find my house and "get me."

By May I had begun to experience numerous stress-related ailments, and I had to admit that I was at the breaking point, both mentally and physically. Finally, two days before the school year ended, I resigned.

Throughout that teaching experience I made one fatal flaw.

It had nothing to do with how I taught or related to my students. It had to do with how I related to my friends and fellow teachers. Not once did I tell anyone what I was experiencing. I was either too proud or too ashamed to admit my problems, so I tried in vain to survive the battle on my own.

I lost. The whole ordeal was not an entire loss, though, because in the months of healing that followed my resignation I learned two invaluable lessons. *God does not intend for us to fight our battles alone. It's no sin to admit that occasionally life hands us more than we can possibly bear on our own.*

God does not intend for us to fight our battles alone. When the mighty warrior grew weary, he allowed his men to fight the battle *for* him, not just *with* him. Had I only set aside my pride I would have discovered numerous teachers and friends ready and willing to offer strength and support.

When the giants of life become too difficult to handle, we can either try to tough it out on our own, or we can accept the strength and encouragement of family and friends. *It's no sin to admit that occasionally life hands us more than we can possibly bear alone.* The sin occurs when we refuse to accept the help that God provides through the people around us.

The apostle Paul knew that we would need that kind of strength to fight life's giants so he instructed us: "Bear ye one another's burdens" (Gal. 6:2, KJV). In so doing, he said, we will be fulfilling Christ's command.

Since completing that stressful teaching position I've made it a point to follow Paul's instructions. I'm no longer afraid to admit my weaknesses and limitations. Instead, I willingly ask my family and friends for their help in carrying the burdens that life hurls my way. Only then am I able to conquer giants and walk into battle with the assurance of victory.

Whether we consider ourselves weaklings or warriors, God's

message is simple. The examples in His Word are clear. We're in the battle of life together. We need each other. We need the strength and support of people around us. And we shouldn't hesitate to ask for it. God never intended for us to face life's giants alone.

25

Make It a Good Day

A group of college students recently returned home for their summer vacations and promptly went into shock. Their quiet, easygoing, slow-paced hometown didn't hold the excitement of campus life. While dorm life was still buzzing at 2:00 in the morning, life back on the farm shut down around 9:30 or 10:00 PM. It was just a matter of days before the students began mumbling and grumbling, "We're bored. There's nothing for us to do."

Being bored is not a new phenomenon for the college students. They mumbled the same complaints years earlier when, as children, their parents surrounded them with hundreds and thousands of dollars' worth of toys: books, puzzles, dolls and dollhouses, trains and train stations, paints, colors, games, swings, and slides. But even then, amidst such paraphernalia, they pulled on their mothers' skirts and whined, "We're bored. There's nothing for us to do."

What a dismal display of boredom! What a lack of initiative! But before we come down too hard on children and young people, let's take a peek inward. We just might see a little of ourselves. Do any of these situations sound familiar?

• Dirty laundry, dirty dishes, grumpy children.

- Same old office routine: dull, boring, completely unfulfilling. You could do it in your sleep—maybe you have.
- Get up. Go to work. Come home. Eat supper. Watch television. Go to bed. All alone. As Garfield the comic strip cat would say, big fat hairy deal.
- Husband gone to work. Children grown—moved away. They never call. Housework is done—doesn't take long when there's no one at home to mess things up. There's nothing to do.
- Retirement. It's not what it's cracked up to be. Money's scarce. Body is tired. Too much time: not enough to do.

The situations may vary here and there but the outcome is the same. Day by day, life slips through our fingers while we go through the motions of living. And if we're not careful, countless golden opportunities to really *live* life and *give* life may go by completely unnoticed.

David Hartman, host of ABC's *Good Morning America* for eleven years, concluded each episode by telling his viewers: "go out and make it a good day." Notice he said to *make* it a good day rather than *have* a good day.

Good days rarely happen on their own. It's almost impossible to sit back and watch a good day just fall into place. That's about as likely to happen as it is for a body to lose weight and get into good physical condition without a diet and exercise. There's more to it than that.

Our attitudes and involvement in the events around us play a major role in the outcome of a day. While we often have no control over the actions of other people and circumstances which influence us, we do have control over our reactions.

Many times we have the power to make a situation good or evil simply by how we respond to it. The writer of Proverbs tells us, "He who seeks good finds good will,/but evil comes to him who searches for it" (11:27).

We've all known people who search for evil. They are never happy. Life is never fair. Nothing is ever right. If they don't have much money they feel deprived. If they do have money, they feel guilty for having more than someone else. If they're sick, they wonder what they did wrong to deserve such punishment. When they're well, they live in fear of getting sick. They silently plead for public praise. But when a pat on the back is given for a job well done, they refuse to graciously accept the compliment.

If you look hard enough, you'll find evil in almost any situation. But the opposite is also true. "He who seeks good finds good will." And how does a person go about seeking good? Consider these three possibilities:

First, remember that each day is filled with God's blessings. We just often fail to recognize them. So begin the day by praying, "Lord, I know You're going to bless me today. Please help me to see You at work." And then, keep your eyes open and consciously look for God's hand in your life. You'll be amazed at the number of blessings you'll see. As an added benefit, the air of expectancy will put a lift in your day as you watch for God, knowing that He's going to bless.

A second way to seek good is to say, "OK. Life seems pretty dull today. How can I spice up someone else's life? How can I make someone else's day a good day?" Take note: you can't help make someone else's day a good day without making your own day better. The two go hand in hand.

Finally, when a situation appears to be negative, take a good, long look at the facts. Then determine how you can either change the facts or modify your attitude to make the situation a positive one.

I once read of a woman who did not own a clothes dryer or

a dishwasher. Since she was not financially able to change those two facts, she modified her attitude. She began thanking God for the sweet smell of clothes dried by the fresh air and sunshine and for the extra time she and her husband had to visit as they washed the supper dishes together. Now there's a lady who sought for good and found it.

Remember, Proverbs promises that if you'll seek for God's blessings you will find them. Don't miss a single opportunity. They're there to be given and enjoyed. Now, "go out and make it a good day."

26

Just Getting By

• Tom glanced at his desk calendar and quickly calculated the number of days until he was scheduled to close a big deal. "If I can just survive the next three weeks I'll have it made."

• Susan sank into a chair after wrestling her two young children to bed. "If I can just get through this terrible toddler stage without losing my sanity I'll have it made."

• Michael stared bleary eyed at the stack of books and notes spread before him. He'd spent the entire weekend studying but he needed at least six more hours of preparation before he'd be ready for the exam. "If I can just pass this economics final I'll have it made."

Can you identify with any of these situations? We've all been in their shoes. In fact, many people live their entire lives with that same attitude. "If I can just make it to Friday . . . If I can just get that promotion . . . If I can just get through law school . . . If I can just get married . . . If I can just land that job . . . If I can just get these loans paid off . . ."

The danger does not necessarily lie in the desire to "have it made" but in the amount of life that is sacrificed in order to reach that point. When we try to live through difficult situations with the attitude of *just getting by,* we tend to live all of life in that same fashion—*just getting by.*

Several years ago I taught high school in a metropolitan suburb. Day after day the routine was pretty much the same.

Students obediently completed tests and assignments in order to pass a course or to be eligible for the athletic program.

Attendance secretaries mechanically kept track of who was where in order to comply with state laws.

Many of the teachers had lost their zeal for education and consequently dragged themselves through their daily routines.

All of us—students, secretaries, and teachers alike—kept ourselves going by clinging to one common thought: *If I can just make it to Friday.*

Meanwhile, life marched on virtually unnoticed. The seasons changed from one glorious spectacle into another. Friendships were born while others died. All around us were opportunities to become involved in other people's lives. But while life marched on, we missed most of it because we were busy striving to "make it to Friday." We were trying to *just get by.*

Christ never intended for Christians to live life *just getting by.* He didn't suffer and die in order for us to simply get from one point of mediocrity to another. What a miserable existence that would be!

Christ's desire is that we have abundant life. His intention is not to merely preserve life but to instill life into every moment of every day. The *Williams New Testament* says, "I have come for people to have life and have it till it overflows" (John 10:10).

Living life that overflows is a far cry from *just getting by.* It's seeing God's hand at work in our daily routines. It's recognizing His blessings that so often go unnoticed. It's finding opportunities to praise Him in the midst of boredom or pain.

Living abundant, overflowing lives is Christ's intention for all of His followers. But we must be on guard, ever alert for the thieves that wait to slowly siphon the strength and joy from our lives.

Just who are these thieves? They are too numerous to count, but here are just a few. One thief is the belief that it doesn't matter how you get there just as long as you get there. Those who buy that lie see only the diploma, the promotion, or the sale. As a result they simply exist from one moment until the next, missing out on all of life, while they wait for the end result to occur.

Another thief is society's spiel that declares life must be lived at breakneck speed if it is to be worth living at all. It's no wonder that those individuals who believe that lie soon find themselves trying to *just get by*.

A third thief is often our own perverted notion that we must live our lives like other people live theirs. We struggle to gain what someone else has rather than receiving the life that Jesus Christ has to offer. In an attempt to measure up to someone else we soon meet ourselves coming and going and eventually resort to *just getting by*.

Often, before we realize what's happening, the thieves of life have begun sapping and stealing. And the result is always the same, regardless of the thief. We slowly slip into a routine of *just getting by*. No longer do we see God's smile in the sunrise or His hand in the affairs of our day. We fail to see the blessings He sends our way because we're concentrating on *just getting by*.

Several years ago a friend called to congratulate me on the birth of my daughter. We talked for a few minutes about the joys of our little girls, mine a few weeks old and his in her twenties. And then he gave me some advice that has proven invaluable.

"Deanna," he said, "don't ever wish away a single moment of your little girl's life. Don't try to hurry her from one stage into the next because every stage is wonderful. I'm now enjoying knowing my little girl as a married adult and this stage is just as special as all of the rest."

My friend's advice has been a great source of help as our family has experienced the usual stages of colic, teething, and temper tantrums. Throughout each moment I've made a conscious effort to not wish away any part. Though the tantrums weren't barrels of fun, had I wished them away and tried to *just get by* I would have missed out on many precious moments that memories are made of.

That's the way life is. In order to live it to the fullest, as Christ intended for us to do, we must live each moment, good and bad, terrific and testing. We must refuse to *just get by* and make a concerted effort to see God in every situation. Only then will we live lives that overflow.

27

Trading Places

If you could trade places with any television character, past or present, who would it be? Captain Kirk from *Star Trek?* Jim Phelps from *Mission Impossible?* Jennifer of *Hart to Hart* fame? Or what about Blake or Krystal Carrington from *Dynasty?*

Personally, I would trade places with Audra Barkley of *The Big Valley,* my all-time favorite Western. Now that show had elegance and class! Audra's family was involved in mining, shipping, ranching, and anything else that was financially profitable. Known throughout California for their influence and wealth, the Barkleys lived in a grand, Southern-style mansion. You know the kind: luscious green landscape, massive white columns, sprawling staircase with mahogany banister, glistening chandeliers—the whole nine yards.

I wouldn't trade places with Audra Barkley just because of her house, even if Silas the butler did do all of the cooking, cleaning, and laundry. No, she can keep the house. It's her wardrobe that I want.

The fashion designers of the 1870s shared my definition of femininity. Full-flowing dresses with skirts in two flounces; dresses of taffeta trimmed with pleats, fringe, and large ribbon bows; petticoats trimmed with tucks, lace insertions, and edging; bonnets trimmed with feathers, flowers, and embroidered gauze—these were the epitome of elegance. They were gorgeous, simply gorgeous.

I would love to trade places with Audra Barkley and spend my days entertaining guests in her Southern mansion while wearing her incredible wardrobe of satin and silk. In no time I'd be known as the fashion plate of California.

I know what you're thinking: *what a silly fantasy!* But once in a while we all dream of trading places with someone whose life appears better than our own. Like Beth, who lives in a beautiful home in a prestigious neighborhood: she dresses her children like minature models, has a full-time maid, and drives the latest-style automobiles.

Or George, the single business executive who collects old cars: classics is what he calls them. He also dabbles in real estate and enjoys a full membership at the racquetball club.

Then there's Karla: she always looks like she just stepped out of *Vogue* magazine. Bright, crisp, new; always the latest in fashion; downright perfect—her wardrobe is unbelievable.

While Karla's wardrobe is unbelievable, so is her debt. While George enjoys his cars, real estate, and health club, he doesn't enjoy his high-pressure job which provides the necessary income for his hobbies. For Beth to have a nice house, new vehicles, and a maid, her husband must frequently work eighty and ninety hours a week to make ends meet.

There's a lot more to other people's lives than what we see. Rarely do we get past the surface niceties and into their daily realities. We usually see the benefits without realizing what they cost. We see prestige but not underlying pressure, an attractive life-style but not aching loneliness, fame but not failures, material "blessings" but not mounting bills, and success but not suffering.

Perhaps the greatest danger in desiring to trade places with other people is not that we don't see their negatives but that we begin to envy their positives. We focus on what they have that we want and in the process we forget to note our own blessings. Proverbs 14:30 warns that this kind of envy "rots the bones."

Edward is the perfect example of rotting envy in progress. He envied his best friend's job, house, and car. He even envied what his best friend ate. Edward lost his appetite whenever his best friend had fried chicken for Sunday lunch and all he had was tuna-fish salad.

The cancerous envy showed its ugly head most vividly the day Edward's first child was born. There were no grandsons on either his side of the family or on his wife's side. (Of course, his best friend had two sons.) Edward wanted a little boy so badly he couldn't think of anything else. He had already invested a small fortune in balls, bats, and toy soldiers. He insisted on decorating the baby's room in blue.

Then the long-awaited day arrived. After many long hours of labor, Edward's child was born. Shortly afterward, he made his way to the waiting room where his family and friends had gathered. With unmistakable disgust and disappointment Edward flatly stated, "Well, we got a girl."

To this day Edward still does not realize how blessed he is to have a loving wife, a steady income, and three precious, healthy little girls. He's convinced that God has something against him while his best friend is God's special pet.

The desire to trade places with other people, if not kept under constant control, can rapidly lead to rotting, malignant envy. Our eyes begin spending more and more time focused on what others possess and less time on our own blessings. Our vision becomes blurred as we see only the positives and none of the negatives. Before long, our perspective is so out of kilter that our spirits begin to rot. What a pitiful picture of a child of God.

Now that I think about it, I don't want to trade places with Audra Barkley after all. She can keep her mansion and her elegant wardrobe. Her clothes may have been spectacular but the California sun can be sizzling. *The Big Valley* takes place a hundred years or so before air conditioners became commonplace. I'd die in the heat. So thanks, but no thanks. I believe I'll stay right where I am.

28

Seeing Through the
Eyes of Love

Have you ever noticed how many people are sad, depressed, grumpy, and just generally out-of-sorts? What a drag! Why don't they think positively, pick themselves up by their bootstraps, and get on with life?

That's the way many people feel toward those struggling individuals who are fighting one or more of life's battles—and losing. Expecting those who hurt to simply think positively is the easy way out for us.

When we demand that people who suffer "grin and bear it," we make a futile attempt to relieve ourselves of our responsibility to minister through love and compassion. Requiring others to pick themselves up by their bootstraps, so to speak, frees us from becoming involved in the nitty-gritty reality of people's lives.

But an attitude of "pick yourself up, Buddy" wasn't exactly the attitude of Christ. Jesus always looked past the exterior to the hurts buried beneath the surface. He had compassion for people in spite of their illness or poverty. He touched them where they hurt regardless of their prestigious positions or tarnished reputations.

Christ never hesitated to become involved in the lives of people who needed Him. He never waited for someone else to act first. It didn't bother Him to get His hands dirty or His feet wet. He didn't care what the social and religious snobs said about Him.

Christ's concern was for people who hurt physically, emotionally, mentally, and spiritually. He saw the hurts when no one else did, for He saw people through His eyes of love.

Seeing through the eyes of love: that's the key to compassion. My niece was just five years old when she taught me what it meant to have such Christlike vision.

One evening Andreana met the neighbors' Saint Bernard: Sam. I was sure that his immense size would frighten her, but it didn't. Instead she peered through the chain-link fence and intently studied his enormous, mournful eyes. For several minutes she continued to gaze into Sam's eyes as she struggled to understand his sadness.

Finally, Andreana came to a conclusion. The reason Sam was sad, she said, was due to his size. Because he was so enormous, she explained, people were afraid. Since they were afraid, Sam had no one to play with him. Andreana summed up Sam's sadness in a nutshell: he was lonely.

Seeing through the eyes of love: it's a whole new vision. It's Christ's vision. With eyes of love we can reach out with compassion to those who hurt because we will actually see their needs. When we see through eyes of love, we can help pick people up rather than putting them down.

While some people have needs that are obvious such as illness or poverty, other people have needs that are less visible to the human eye. People in this group need our compassion as much as anyone else, but they're harder to detect.

People with less-visible needs often don't want others to know that they have problems and pains. They go to great lengths to hide behind deceitful masks and frozen smiles. Some pretend to be cheerful and positive about the whole world. Their standard answer for "How are you?" is: "Couldn't be better!" When asked about a particular situation they quickly reply, "Things are going great, just great!"

Perhaps the writer of Proverbs had these people in mind when he wrote, "Even in laughter the heart may ache,/and joy may end in grief" (14:13).

Still other people who hide behind masks do so in order to distract from the real problems of their lives. They're like the little boy who came home from school one day and said, "Mom, I've got a big problem. My teacher told me I have to start writing legibly, but if I do she'll find out that I can't spell!"

Though their needs are harder to detect, these folks need our love and compassion just as much as those who boldly call out for help.

Whether it's frozen smiles, illegible handwriting, bizarre clothes and hairstyles, loud obnoxious behavior, or some other mask, it requires special vision to see beyond the facade. We must be willing to get our hands dirty, our feet wet, and our hearts involved in compassionate concern.

But in order to minister with such compassion, we must see the real needs and the human pain. We must see others as Christ sees them. We must see them through His eyes of love.

29

The Builder's Tool

His name was Joseph. Not the boy with the multicolored coat, not the male-counterpart of the famous couple from Nazareth, not the one of Arimathea in whose tomb Christ was buried. This Joseph was a builder. He built character. He built self-confidence. He built strong individuals.

Joseph's powerful tool for building lives was encouragement. In fact, he was so busy mending and strengthening other people that his friends called him Barnabas which meant "Son of Encouragement." (See Acts 4:36.) Barnabas simply couldn't resist encouraging the people around him.

Take the great apostle Paul, for example. His previous dealings with the followers of Christ had been so deathly brutal that even after his dynamic conversion experience the other believers were skeptical of him. In fact, when Paul arrived in Jerusalem he was not welcomed with open arms by the Christian community. Instead, he was rejected out of doubt and fear.

But Barnabas stood beside Paul. In his calm, convincing manner Barnabas introduced Paul to the apostles and encouraged them to accept him as a genuine believer. (See Acts 9:27.)

It was Barnabas who gave his cousin John Mark a second chance to travel with him on a missionary journey even though John Mark had deserted him on an earlier trip. As a result of being given a second chance, John Mark continued ministering in the early church and eventually wrote the account of Christ's life that we know as the Gospel of Mark.

Barnabas—an encourager: one who knows how to refresh weary hearts, boost discouraged spirits, and believe when no one else believes.

Everyone needs a Barnabas—at least one. I've been blessed with several, like Ramona Miller, Chuck Choate, and Mike Moorehead—all teachers who had no idea that I would one day become a professional writer. Like my best friend and husband, Scott, who has never resented the fact that I don't use my college degree to bring home a steady income. Instead he finds countless ways to show his love and support for my work.

Perhaps more important than having a Barnabas, though, is being one. Barnabas literally changed the course of people's lives through his words of encouragement. We, too, can have a tremendous impact on the lives of those around us just by speaking much-needed words of support and praise.

Mrs. Beneduci was a teacher who, many years ago, changed the course of a nine-year-old boy's life. Stevie was smart and bright. Everyone knew that. But Mrs. Beneduci was more concerned with another one of Stevie's abilities: his keen sense of hearing. Even though he could not see, he could detect sounds when no one else heard them. Day after day, Mrs. Beneduci encouraged Stevie to use his incredible gift. And he did.

Because of his elementary-school teacher's consistent encouragement, Stevie continued to develop his gifted ears. Eventually, he became one of secular music's greatest artists. His ability as a singer, songwriter, and producer earned him five Grammy awards in 1975, not to mention numerous gold singles, gold albums, and platinum records. Because of the encouragement of one woman, music lovers today continue to enjoy the creative genius of Stevie Wonder.

So, how about it? Are you interested in being a Barnabas ... a Mrs. Beneduci ... an encourager? If so, begin by putting these six steps into practice today.

• Be aware of people's needs. Look for them, take note of them, and write them down. Don't assume for a moment that someone doesn't need encouraging.

• Pray for wisdom to know how to meet people's needs through words and deeds of encouragement. Many times the most effective moments of encouragement are the result of prayerful thought and advance preparation.

• Practice encouraging others by complimenting numerous people every day, strangers as well as friends. For most of us, the ability to be an encourager is not inherited. It must be deliberately developed if it is to ever become a natural part of our lives.

• Compile a list of ways you can encourage people in various situations such as cards, letters, flowers, food, and phone calls.

• Whenever possible, keep in contact with the people you encourage. For example, if you've sent a note of encouragement concerning someone's job interview, follow up with a phone call to let the person know you were genuinely interested.

• Remember that an encourager builds character, self-confidence, and stronger individuals. Signs of improvement are often not immediately evident. In fact, many times you may never know how you've affected another person's life.

I can honestly say that the course of my life changed the night my husband surprised me with a new Smith-Corona typewriter and encouraged me to follow my dream to become a writer. All I needed was one person who firmly believed in me. I thank God for my Barnabas.

Encouragement: it's an amazing, powerful tool. It builds

character. It inspires dreams. It boosts heavy hearts and lifts weary shoulders. Encouragement energizes, excites, and reassures. It can literally change the course of a human life.

Whose life will you change today?

30

Sidetracked

Sidetracked: the condition which occurs when something is supposed to happen but doesn't, due to diversionary circumstances.

We all get sidetracked from time to time—like the day when my husband washed the car, mowed the lawn, cleaned out the garage, and repaired the stereo. All those things were great accomplishments, but in reality they were diversionary tactics. He had originally set aside the day to paint the master bedroom —a job which he thoroughly dreaded.

• Like the woman who made a "quick trip" to the store to buy her son a pair of blue jeans and wound up looking at the new spring fashions for more than two hours.

• Like the high school student who spent an entire evening reading a novel for English class. His mother thought it was a miraculous event since the book report wasn't due for three weeks. The student's sudden love for Steinbeck, however, was just a diversionary tactic. He had a geometry exam coming up the next morning, and he would do anything in order to avoid studying geometry.

Getting sidetracked is an inevitable part of life. Many times we get sidetracked due to events beyond our control. The phone rings, unexpected guests arrive at the front door, the kitchen sink springs a leak, or a thunderstorm blows in. We simply can't stick with our planned schedule, and it's not our fault.

But there are other times when we either consciously or subconsciously choose an alternate route to the one we know we should follow. For example, when the West Texas dust is so thick on the furniture that Scott begins writing notes in it, I know that it's time to dust.

But I detest dusting. It's a hopeless cause: a pointless activity out here in the dust bowl. Invariably, on those days when I've set aside time to clean the furniture and baseboards, I usually accomplish a great many other tasks. I wash the laundry, scrub the shower, and clean out the attic. At the end of the day the house still needs dusting but, my goodness, look at all I got done!

Therein lies the dilemma. The tricky thing about getting sidetracked is that often the things we do as a result of being sidetracked are good things. Who could possibly fault me for cleaning the shower or washing laundry? And what woman in her right mind would dare complain that her husband mowed the lawn or cleaned out the garage?

While we're at it, there's certainly nothing wrong with attending week-night Bible studies, teaching a Sunday School class, serving on church or community service committees, playing softball on the church team, being a volunteer counselor, sponsoring the youth on summer trips, singing in the church choir, or regularly attending church services on Sundays and Wednesdays.

There's nothing wrong with those activities *unless* we've gotten sidetracked from the purpose God has for our individual lives.

Where does God fit into all of our activities? How often do we have difficulty finding time to spend alone with Him because of all the good, wholesome, spiritual things we are involved in?

One Sunday evening as I drove out of my driveway I noticed that my unsaved neighbors were working in their front yard. *I really should stop and visit with them,* I thought. But the evening worship service began in fifteen minutes and I was already running late, so I hurried on.

Somehow I think God would have been more pleased if I had been late or missed the service entirely. But I got sidetracked from His purpose for me at that moment by something good. After all, who could fault me for going to church?

Avoiding getting sidetracked is not an easy task because it requires clearly knowing God's purpose for our individual lives. It requires the determined ability to say no to good opportunities when they conflict with God's direction. It requires having the ability to make proper choices.

It wasn't easy, but even Christ had to carefully make proper decisions in order to avoid being sidetracked. Imagine all of the people Christ did *not* heal. When His ministry on earth was completed and He returned to heaven, disease and death were still a part of human life. Yet, in order to minister as God directed Him, Christ had to bypass some needs so He could tend to others.

Consider all the lessons that Christ did *not* teach. He knew full well that the earth was round, but He never told anyone that. He knew what Orville and Wilbur Wright would not discover for nearly two thousand years. Yet He never shared that knowledge. Why? Because He knew He had only a few brief years in which to carry out God's purpose for His life. He couldn't afford to get sidetracked.

Perhaps one of the reasons we are often so easily sidetracked is our notion that if a job needs to be done then we must be the ones to do it. Yet there are always jobs to be done, and when we attempt to do them all we soon get sidetracked from the ones God means for us to carry out.

Christ knew which jobs belonged to Him. He recognized His responsibilities and focused His attentions and energies on them. Amazingly enough, He left all the other jobs up to folks like you and me. He only had time to do what God had called Him to do.

Christ was keenly aware of the responsibilities God had given to Him. He couldn't afford to get sidetracked, not even for a moment, not even by something good. Neither can we.

31

Safe and Secure

I am not a courageous person. While I prefer to think of myself as cautious, what it boils down to is: I'm a basic coward. Adventure has never been in my bones. Chicken Little had nothing on me. Perhaps a true story will help you get the picture.

Being the youngest of three girls, some folks would say that my precollege years were just a tad on the sheltered side. Aside from the fact that I had never put gas in my car or started a lawn mower before I was twenty-one years old—I was twenty-three before I ever spent an entire night alone—it was an experience I'll never forget.

Shortly before my husband left for his overnight trip, which was the cause of my solitude, we invested in a small sonar burglar alarm. Our theory was that when I went to bed I would place the alarm outside the bedroom door and turn it on. The alarm would then send out a beam which, if it were broken by an intruder, would cause the alarm to sound. This, we thought, would give me a feeling of security.

Believing that I would be fine without him, Scott left town one Thursday morning and I went to work. I was not quite so convinced about my safety. After all, I had seen numerous movies, watched the ten-o'clock news, and read countless magazine articles about women who were mugged, attacked, killed, and so forth. In every case, the women had been alone. That did it. I knew I would not live to see another day.

But if indeed it was my turn to die, I refused to go without a good fight. Upon arriving home from work I thoroughly investigated inside every cabinet and closet, behind doors and curtains, and under every large piece of furniture. *You never know where someone might be hiding,* I told myself.

Finally, convinced that no one was waiting to play out the shower scene from *Psycho,* I checked and rechecked every door and window to be certain they were secure. Then, just to be sure, I jammed folding chairs under each doorknob. By the time I finished, the house was secure enough for the president himself to sleep there . . . alone!

Now I'm sure that all of this sounds extremely ridiculous to you, as it does to me now. But you must keep in mind that I had never spent a night alone, yet I was blessed with a vivid imagination—an imagination that easily kicked into overtime at the slightest hint of fear.

By now you may also be wondering why in the world I didn't just spend the night with a friend. No, though the thought had crossed my mind, I was determined to survive the night alone. It was time to grow up, even if it killed me.

After hours of mindless television programs, I decided to turn in. Finally, after rechecking every door one more time and setting the burglar alarm, I went to bed. My mind, however, stayed up to roam throughout the darkened house, peeking behind curtains and under chairs.

Wide awake, ears perked to detect every noise, I soon discovered one minor problem in my self-secured house. Every time the central heating unit kicked on, the sudden air flow set off the alarm. Thus began a tense night of anxiously waiting for the shrill blast to sound or the burglar to attack.

By dawn I was convinced that I had spent a silly, sleepless

night. Nothing I had done, absolutely none of my precautions had given me a sense of security. That kind of security comes from only one source: our Heavenly Father.

Isaiah 26:3 says, "Thou wilt keep him in perfect peace, whose mind is stayed on thee: because he trusteth in thee" (KJV). We can take some precautions and use our common sense but ultimately only God can give us peace and security.

The key is a mind that is focused on God. For people like me with overactive imaginations it takes more than avoiding certain thoughts. It requires hard work. It takes dedicated determination to retrain an imaginative mind. Positive thoughts must replace the negative, frightening ones. Over the recent years I've found two thought-training activities to be particularly helpful.

First of all, reciting Scripture is an extremely powerful method of forcing our minds in the proper direction. The Psalms literally brim with words about God's protection and care. When David's life was endangered by the Philistines, he said, "When I am afraid,/I will trust in you./. . . in God I trust; I will not be afraid./What can man do to me?" (56:3,11).

A second way to fight frightening thoughts is to pray about whoever or whatever pops to mind. On nights when sleep has refused to come, I've found myself praying for people I haven't thought of in years—an elementary school playmate or someone I once worked with in a summer job. I eventually drift into a calm, peaceful sleep because my thoughts have been focused on my Heavenly Father.

Fears come from numerous areas of our lives. Maybe it's an illness or an upcoming surgery. Perhaps it is the fear of losing a loved one and being left alone. Family, friends, finances, regrets, responsibilities, retirement—almost anything can cause fear, especially late at night when the noise of the world steps out and the quiet of the stillness slips in. Regardless of the source of fear, God in His infinite wisdom has assured us of His peace when we fix our thoughts on Him.

Recently I noticed an ad in *Reader's Digest* for a home-security alarm system. The caption read, "Happiness is knowing my family's safe at home." No, happiness is knowing that our security rests in the hands of our Almighty Father. Our lives are in *His* hands.

Many years have passed since that first frightful night. I'm happy to say that time and experience have proven to be great teachers. After spending numerous nights alone I can now confidently say with the psalmist, "I will lie down and sleep in peace,/for you alone, O Lord,/make me dwell in safety" (Ps. 4:8). With that knowledge, I can focus my thoughts on Him and enjoy His perfect peace. No alarm system in the world can provide that kind of security.

32

And Then Came Jonathan

Once the hours between 11:00 PM and 7:00 AM were reserved for sleeping.

Then came Jonathan. Now the two of us watch old movies and reruns at two o'clock in the morning.

Once the third bedroom of our house served as my office. A floor lamp, rolltop desk, computer table, swivel chair, and filing cabinet were all perfectly arranged. The closet was lined with shelves where my books stood at attention, ready for immediate use.

Then there was Jonathan. My office is now a nursery decorated in clowns, and the closet shelves are loaded with socks, shoes, terry cloth sleepers, play clothes, toys, diapers, blankets, and crib sheets. My husband must now maneuver around my office furniture to get to our bed, and the majority of my library is in storage.

Once the fragrance of various perfumes could be subtly sensed in my hair and clothing.

Then Jonathan was born. Now the scent of baby formula follows me wherever I go.

Once I could wear my blue jeans without giving up the pleasure of breathing. The decision of what to wear each morning depended only upon the day's activities and my mood.

But Jonathan came. Now my wardrobe consists of bulky sweaters and articles made with elastic waistbands.

It would be an understatement to simply say that Jonathan has changed my life. I no longer have a child: I have children. I must help my daughter learn how to be a sister. She and I must now share our time with another person while her daddy is at work. I, being the youngest of three girls, am still trying to figure out what to do with a baby boy.

Jonathan truly has changed my life—in many ways. Some of the changes have come about only through sacrifice. But on those days when I'm tempted to ask for sympathy there's a surefire remedy that puts everything back into perspective. I simply hold my son. Everything else fades away in the presence of his deep-blue eyes, innocent grin, and soft gentle coos.

There's another Man who has changed my life. But His demands are even greater than those of my son. I sacrifice my time, money, and energy for Him, but He wants even more.

He wants me to look the other way when someone offends me. I must ignore the temptation to get even.

He wants me to consider other people's desires before my own. I must quit looking out for my own interests and trust Him with my wants and needs.

He wants me to be merciful and forgiving. I must not only forgive but I'm also supposed to love the people who hurt me.

He wants me to give what I have to help people who are in need. Whatever is required—food, money, clothing, time, love —I must share it with those who need it, no strings attached.

He wants *me*—all of me. He wants my very life. This, certainly, is the greatest sacrifice He asks me to make for Him. To give Him my very life, I must be willing to do anything He requires, even to die.

Once again the sacrifices seem great. To those who do not know the Man, they seem highly unreasonable. Quite honestly, there are times in my human frailty that I cry out to Him, "You're not fair! I can't possibly do . . . give . . . go . . . say . . . forget . . . forgive . . . You ask too much!"

The sacrifices often seem great. Indeed, at times they *are* great. When I focus on the sacrifices alone, they begin to appear unreasonable and eventually unbearable.

The remedy, however, is simple. It's the same one I use with my son. I look at the face of the One who requires the sacrifice.

Whenever I'm quite sure that I've forgiven more times than anyone else and given more of myself than humanly possible, all I have to do is look at the face of my Lord, the One who requires so much of me. Suddenly, in His presence, in the light of His supreme sacrifice, my little bit of giving and forgiving don't seem like much after all.